A Different Place

"Daryl exposes truths in God's word like no one else I know. What others brush over, Daryl digests and communicates as 'anchors of truth' that I can confidently attach my life to. *A Different Place* can truly take you to a different place in your spiritual walk."

GREG INGRAM, BUSINESS OWNER
TUCSON, ARIZONA

"There are precious few Christian men who are totally committed to studying and applying God's word in their daily living. Daryl Kraft is a tremendous student of the word and a reliable disciple we can look to for advice and wise counsel. In his latest book, *A Different Place*, he shares some unique insights about what a 'grace-filled' life looks like."

DR. JAMES GRASSI, AUTHOR-NATIONAL SPEAKER
POST FALLS, IDAHO

"*A Different Place*, honestly speaking, is one of the best books I have ever read for Christian believers. It is a book that speaks some serious biblical truth! It magnifies God and makes man look appropriately small!"

EDDY HANCOCK, COLLEGE STUDENT
MOSCOW, IDAHO

"I believe that Divine inspiration led Daryl Kraft to produce his new book *A Different Place*. In my view, it is one of the most important books ever written. This significant contribution is a thoughtful, and thought provoking, approach to faith and belief. His insightful and objective analysis will indeed take you to *A Different Place*."

BUCK JOHNSTON, MASTER OF AGRICULTURE
AGRICULTURAL AND NATURAL RESOURCES RECLAMATION SPECIALIST

"I recently finished reading Daryl Kraft's new book *A Different Place*. His own testimony throughout the book was so honest and it described me perfectly. For many years I have felt enslaved to living the 'victorious Christian life' and being perfect in the eyes of other Christians. Yet I knew that I was anything but perfect and this almost destroyed my relationship with my wife, family, and friends. But praise God, the foundational truths in this book shattered this bondage!"

STEPHEN BRYANT, BUSINESS OWNER
GREENSBORO, NORTH CAROLINA

"The reader will find that this book, *A Different Place*, reawakens and reinforces truths that are basic to our Christian walk. Yet how easily we forget them (or ignore them) and find ourselves trying to help God."

RICHARD PENN,
HAYDEN, IDAHO

Testimonials regarding

The Businessman's Guide to Real Success

"Driven by discontent with life commonly lived in two separate worlds (spiritual and business), Daryl Kraft is unwilling to shrink from the claims of Christ in all dimensions of his life. The *Businessman's Guide* chronicles experiences that have fueled Daryl's passion for Christ-honoring excellence in business and integrity of heart."

DR. DENNIS DIRKS, DEAN
TALBOT SCHOOL OF THEOLOGY, CALIFORNIA

"The life-changing truths that God has given to Daryl in this book have given me the handles in life to be the husband, father, and businessman God desires. Nothing else has impacted my life in such a way as these life-giving truths from God's Word."

BEN EVANS, BUSINESS OWNER
SACRAMENTO, CALIFORNIA

"This book is a must for men."

NIMROD McNAIR, PRESIDENT
McNAIR ASSOCIATES, INC., GEORGIA

"Daryl Kraft is a man that walks his talk. This is a book you will read and read again."

TERRY GNIFFKE, PRESIDENT
CALIBER HOME SERVICES, INC., CALIFORNIA

Testimonies regarding

Daryl Kraft and his ministry

"Through Daryl's sharing of God's wisdom and work in his life, I have come to love my life, my wife, my career, and most of all, Jesus. No other man, in my time, has had more impact upon my spiritual life, my marriage, my career, and my ministry to others."

JONATHAN HANKS, BUSINESS OWNER
COLUMBUS, OHIO

"I have met men in athletics, in ministry, and in the business world. I've known very few with the integrity and commitment to blend Jesus Christ into their environment with more dedication than Daryl Kraft."

REV. JOHN WERHAS, PASTOR (AND FORMER DODGER)
YORBA LINDA FRIENDS CHURCH, CALIFORNIA

"Daryl is someone in whom the Scripture breathes. Again and again he has taught me the power of God's Word to change lives."

JOHN LAMB, BUSINESS OWNER
MADISON, WISCONSIN

"Walking in the 'law of liberty' is quite simply put—living and breathing worship."

MERWIN AND VERA "SCOOTER" SEVERTSON
BIBLE STUDY MEMBERS, COEUR D'ALENE, IDAHO

A SIMPLIFIED LIFE:

Your Career and Life from God's Perspective

Daryl Kraft

living oracles
Hayden, Idaho

A Simplified Life: *Your Career and Life from God's Perspective*

Copyright 2013 by Daryl Kraft

Published by Living Oracles, Inc.
Hayden, Idaho 83835
www.livingoracles.com

Cover and interior design by Kimberly Martin

Living Oracles books are available at special quantity discounts to use as premiums and sales promotions, as book club, Bible study, or edification group selections, or for use in corporate training or incentive programs. For more information, please contact Living Oracles or your local bookstore.

Printed in the United States of America
20 19 18 17 16 15 14 13 12 11 10 9 8 7 6 5 4 3 2 1

Colophon is a registered trademark of Living Oracles, Inc.

Dedication

To Sherryl, and our four children.

For our entire marriage, I have tested my wife's patience through years of building a business and now writing yet another book. For more than fifty years (and raising four children) she has stuck with me through thick and thin, and we have grown together in Christ beyond what I could possibly have dreamed. Today, she is more precious to me than ever, for her encouragement, wisdom, insight, and strength...both in life and in God's word.

It is to her and to our children—Greg, Doug, Kim, and Shelli—that I dedicate this book. They were the ones on the "front lines" of my harsher years. That we now have such a close and loving family together, I can take no credit. I give all the praise and glory for this to our loving God, who has cared for and protected each of us in a multitude of ways that only He fully knows.

Acknowledgments

To the many of you who agreed to read and comment on various drafts of the manuscript, thank you.

To my executive assistant, Penny Bradbury, who tirelessly worked on this project with me over many years, my deepest thanks.

Thanks also to Chris Schneider, my friend and colleague for over 35 years at Environment Control, for providing invaluable insight on the structure and direction of the message.

To Allyson Gross, who edited portions of this book, I give thanks for the patience she displayed in bringing earlier drafts into reality.

To Patrick Adair, my publisher, for his unwavering support.

And to my wife Sherryl, whose insightful questions and keen eye brought immeasurable improvement to the pages of this book.

A SIMPLIFIED LIFE:

Your Career and Life from God's Perspective

In all your ways acknowledge Him, and He shall direct your paths.

PROVERBS 3:6

Contents

Foreword

God directs us in His timing

This book is a perfect example of how God directs us throughout our life in His timing. About twelve years ago, I began a writing project that was essentially this book in concept. The name was different, but the Lord had placed on my heart the idea to share with other business people the core business principles I have learned over the years in starting and growing a national corporation. It was not intended to trumpet that I have "arrived" or as a platform for bragging about being successful. On the contrary, it was a book that mostly shared how I, in my own effort, was completely inadequate to build anything of lasting value.

The more I gathered notes and worked on that manuscript, however, the farther away from its completion I seemed to get. Certain sections simply would not come together in a cohesive way that was satisfying. I now know that this was because God was still working more business and life-experiences *into me* before these topics would become clear in a meaningful way. Short of that growth, the words would ring hollow and formulaic to the reader.

Meanwhile, God was leading me on a wonderful journey in studying His word and in sharing with others a Bible study in Coeur d'Alene, Idaho. Through this time, the Lord led me through experience after experience that had powerful applications for this earlier writing project. But before the manuscript could be completed, He led me to stop working on it for a while and to begin writing on an entirely different subject. That eventually led to publication of a book focused entirely on God and His grace, entitled: *A Different Place (The peace and freedom that comes from knowing: God has done it all…He is all we need)*. It was from a combination of writing *A Different Place*, the experience gained from the Bible study, and more years of experience in the operations of the company that produced in me the remaining essential parts missing in my thinking for the writing of this book. I am now at peace in writing it.

A Simplified Life: Your Career and Life from God's Perspective is the first in an "Out-of-the-Hide" book series that will be published, Lord willing, offering practical guidance on matters of career, business, and life. The title of this series, *Out of the Hide*, comes from a brief conversation I had nearly thirty years ago now, but I never forgot it. On the last day of our company's National Leadership Conference, a businessman who had been associated with Environment Control through the ownership of several of our franchises, came up and told me what he liked about the Environment Control franchise concept: "It's all out of the hide," he said. "Lots of franchise concepts are mostly theory, but yours is based 100% on *real 'out of the hide' experience*. That's what makes it successful." I never forgot that conversation. It became a foundational principle in growing the company to what it is today; everything we offer our franchisees comes out of our experience.

Finally, the release of *A Simplified Life* comes at an auspicious time in Environment Control's history, as the company is celebrating its fiftieth anniversary. May the Lord use it, and the real-life experiences He has given me to share with you within its pages, for His glory (and your personal and business success)!

Phase I:

God's perspective on business and work.

Chapter One:

Transitional Perspective

(From human effort to God's abiding truth)

> *"Man's steps are ordained by the LORD,*
> *How then can man understand his way?"*
>
> PROVERBS 20:24

As a young man still in college, I purchased from a graduating senior his share of a janitorial business. Before long, I bought the balance of the company from the other owner and became the hesitant, but proud, owner of a few run-down pieces of cleaning equipment, some supplies, and six accounts grossing $600.00 per month. From that humble beginning, my wife and I launched a janitorial company called "AAA Building Maintenance Company" (so it would be listed first in the phone book). I was still in college and needed a way to pay the bills.

At the time, as a Christian, I had all kinds of ideas of what being a "Christian businessman" meant, most of which I realize today were erroneous. But during those days I was zealous to proclaim Christ and the gospel through my business. In fact, as part of our business plan, we incorporated the policy of primarily hiring Christian young people from Christian colleges and surrounding local churches to do the cleaning services we offered. We took great care never to discriminate against the non-Christian and we never refused to hire someone who was otherwise qualified, but we did seek to hire from Christian sources whenever possible.

While I was busily building this so-called Christian business, one thing remained crystal clear within me. I had *no* desire to run a janitorial company, Christian or otherwise, for the long run. I only had the urgent need for some monthly income. I wanted to use the company to feed my family long enough to get through school and graduate, then I thought I could unload it on another student in the same way that I had purchased it. Building a janitorial business was the last thing I wanted to do after graduating from college. After all, who wants to use a college degree to clean toilets and empty trash cans for a living?

To be honest, being a janitor made me feel inferior. I wanted a career that was more prestigious (in my eyes), something that would draw the admiration of my parents, family and those who knew me. But there seemed to be no other option to pay my bills. I felt stuck. In time, however, I grew increasingly obsessed with making money. The business became my god and money—my idol. My family was shunted to the back of my priorities as I gave every waking hour to the business. After all, wasn't I doing all of this work and effort for them? I was attracted to all the newest strategic and tactical methodologies to run my company even more successfully. I read the *Wall Street Journal* and *Fortune* magazine religiously, and talked to other businessmen to soak up what was working for them. I cobbled together what I thought were priorities and principles that would continue to build my enterprise. And for years, I followed this human approach to running a business.

I implemented every trick in the book to gain advantage over my competitors. I manipulated endlessly how I could reduce every expense. I would intentionally intimidate my employees into working harder for fear of losing their jobs, which continuously destabilized the office workplace. If an employee made a mistake, I would never forget. If I could hire someone cheaper to do the same job, I fired and hired accordingly. If I could benefit the bottom line in any way, I would take it. When I needed to increase cash flow, I delayed paying vendor's bills, using them as unwilling bankers to float my own cash problems. And to customers, I would say whatever it took to make the sale, regardless of its truthfulness.

Of course, I didn't start out in business with this level of disrespect toward my employees, vendors, and customers. It all developed gradually. My business practices were formed as a result of my humanly devised "wisdom" (some call this business "experience," "discernment," or "acumen"), which I picked up here and there from this or that article, or a news program, or a conversation with another business person, or something I concocted for myself. I perceived these tidbits of information as "solutions" to many of the hard problems I encountered during the day-to-day, rough and tumble activity of running a business.

When you are giving your utmost to develop and manage a service business, balance budgets, keep customers happy, and basically bust your backside every single day, morning to night, to stay in business anyway you can—it often seems like every time you turn around, something is threatening your success. And, for my type "A" perfectionist personality, it was very easy to become angry toward whatever that threat was.

In the service business, if your customer is happy with your work, you rarely get a call telling you about it. But if they are unhappy, you'll be the first to know. In practice, some days seem to be nothing more than dealing with a steady stream of customer complaints. These complaints almost always were the result of an employee letting me down. Such calls were not only embarrassing personally, but risked jeopardizing the company's reputation. If a complaint resulted in losing a customer, then maybe the next complaint would lose another; and the next—another. It was not long before the company's very survival, in my worried and stressed-out mind, was on the line. If I didn't have income from the company, my family would have nothing to live on. I had kids to feed and bills to pay!

And what was the source of all these problems? *People!* Like *employees* who didn't follow through with the job they were trained to do, and some even stealing from me or jeopardizing my entire business by being the cause of a major embarrassment, lawsuit, or a large insurance claim; *key staff* who I had invested time and money, in terms of training and positions of trust, who then would leave and sometimes become my competitor; *vendors*, who would not deliver equipment or supplies when promised, or at the price quoted; and finally, *customers*, who often showed no grace, and at times expected more service than they were willing to pay for.

Also government red tape and regulation were a problem. Just when you thought you had your budgets set so you could squeak out and maintain a reasonable bottomline, you hear that Congress just raised the minimum wage by a dollar. Your brain begins again to race through all of your client budgets knowing that you can't possibly pass that increase on to many of them, thus decreasing your income once again.

Eventually, I burned out. I hated the daily calls from customers, the stress and worry of making payroll and paying bills. I wanted out of this line of work altogether and tried to get out on several occasions. It was far more of a curse than a blessing. Yet there was nowhere else I could go and support my family. My big ego was trapped by golden handcuffs.

Then something interesting happened. Several of my college buddies, who were unsatisfied in their own careers, came to me interested in what I was doing. They asked if I would help them get started in the same business. I counseled with a lawyer, set up Environment Control as a franchising company, and to my mixed surprise and dismay, I soon had five franchises.

At first, I thought this was an answer to prayer. I would finally be able to escape the hassle of running a janitorial business and dealing with all of those unappreciative and negative customers myself. It didn't take me long to realize that all I did, by forming a franchising corporation, was jump from the skillet into the fire. Now I was counseling an increasing number of janitorial businesses on how to navigate the very same problems and complaints from customers that I had become miserable engaging in with one company. I was now dealing with a multitude of businesses, which I had to work even harder to make successful. Each new franchise simply magnified my problems and stress.

All of this stress and anger can slowly build within you like a pressure cooker. In a service business like ours, every aspect of developing and managing a business can be fraught with killer stress. Like many businessmen have shared with me, it is easy to build up anger toward people who you view are continually letting you down. So all of the methods I devised to keep things under control for my individual business, which I shared in previous paragraphs, I tried to share with my franchisees. These were the things I humanly thought were smart and good business, what any businessman must do to survive and succeed.

I was wrong.

All of this effort only led me deeper and deeper into a world of dark despair. The internal stress I felt, on a daily basis, was increasingly beyond my endurance to withstand. The pit of my gut was in continual motion, twisting and churning, like a bubbling cauldron of burning acid. I was a "successful" businessman alright, but the cost for that so-called success, in terms of personal health and family, was a price I could not continue to pay for much longer.

I can honestly say, without risk of being overdramatic, that in those days I felt like I was hanging on to physical life by a piece of frayed thread, and I inwardly feared that the tenuous grip I had on that abused strand was slipping away. The more I struggled to gain control of my circumstances, the more my life seemed to career out of control, both at work and at home. Of course, to the casual observer, my church and family life looked perfect—a flawless façade as an upstanding pillar in the church and God-fearing family man. But inwardly, I was personally "holding it together" every day, not by living the victorious Christian life through faith in God, but by abusing prescription drugs. I routinely ignored my doctor's advice and took six Valium a day—risking overdose—just to make it from morning until night.

As far as my marriage was concerned, what seemed like a match made in heaven only a few years prior, where we could not imagine ever living apart, had now become a hellish prison where we could not imagine living together much longer. I could not talk to my wife about *anything* without the conversation disintegrating into an anger-laced confrontation. Whether it was kids, money, house chores, coming home late from work, even where we might take the kids for a vacation, all were worthy topics to trigger another verbal brawl.

When things could not possibly get any worse … they did. One day I received a call from my mother that my cousin Dave was dying of an aggressive form of cancer. If I wanted to see him before he died, I would need to drop what I was doing and go see him immediately. Dave and I were the same age and had grown up together. We were very close. After graduation, he went into "full-time ministry" and ended up as a pastor, while I went on to college and into business. That call from my mom profoundly jolted my life. Dave was facing the one thing that I was so afraid of: death.

I shared in my last book, *A Different Place*, about my experiences beside Dave's hospital bed, so I will not repeat those details here. For you who read that book, you know that God brought me to a life-altering crossroad in that hospital room. As I stood looking at Dave's transcendently peaceful face, I saw a man who had nothing of the wealth and outward "success" that I had, yet possessed the one thing that my money could not buy: PEACE. God showed me at that moment that Dave had more peace *dying* than I had *living*. He already possessed *in this life* what I had been striving to achieve for years, but had deluded myself into believing was not attainable this side of a future heaven. At least that was the pabulum I fed myself, to appease the nagging mental pain and to endure the stress of my current life.

But by Dave's bed, God exposed all my excuses for what they really were: a toxic brew of lies. At that moment, God's divine truth broke through, like a great beacon of light slicing through darkness. That truth was beyond my human understanding to comprehend, but there it was before me. I was looking at the living proof of God's truth in Dave's face—that the peace of God was not reserved for a future heaven, but was given to us now and in full measure, available for us to experience *in this life*! One thing I saw clearly in that instant: to settle for anything less than God's peace *right now* was to live a lie.

At that moment of truth, while still in a state of mental and physical exhaustion, I prayed the most earnest prayer in my entire life. I poured myself out to God—I silently prayed how I could no longer go on, how I could no longer bear the weight of life, and how I didn't care about any of

it any more. All I yearned for was to know God and experience the peace that Dave was experiencing in Him. I felt
stripped of everything and clung to one solitary desire:

Dear God, I just want to know You!

By God's mercy, I felt the weight of the world begin to
lift off my shoulders in that hospital room. I immediately
understood that this prayer had been different from all the
other prayers of dedication and rededication I had made
over the last twenty years of Christian living. Over the
coming weeks, I felt a new vibrancy and hunger for God's
word. But I also began to worry that I would soon lose this
newfound peace, that it would fade like every other short-
lived emotional surge I had experienced over the years
during that occasional church revival. It brought such concern to me that I grew obsessed with finding the answer to
how I could go on day-by-day from there. What did I need
to do to continue in this sweet fellowship with God?

I racked my brain over the next few days for the answer
to these questions. I thought back to all of the teachings
I had heard for decades, from the pulpit and Bible study
classes, regarding maintaining our relationship with God.
The only thing that came to mind was a recurring theme
I had heard over and over again: that money was the root
of all evil. This was usually shared in the same message
where a tithe, an offering, or some form of sacrificial giving
(of the same evil stuff) was asked for. To be fair, what was
actually taught was that the *love* of money was the root of
all evil, but for me, that nuance was a distinction without
a difference.

That was it, I thought. I had come up with my core problem. Instead of doing what Dave had done by going into

full-time Christian ministry, I had gotten off track by going into business. But now, I could not continue in business if I expected to have a close relationship with God. I could not deal with money, profits, customer complaints, and people disappointments on a daily basis, and then expect to maintain God's abiding peace within. I would need a major transition in my life, a transition that would involve a career change from business to some form of "full-time ministry." After all, everyone knew that the only work that had any real and lasting spiritual value before God was the "sacred" work of full-time pastors, evangelists, and missionaries. Right? I had spent decades nibbling around the edges in Christian service, as an elder to my church and on missionary boards, but it obviously had not been enough. To my thinking, the commitment now had to be all the way. I had to leave business and enter "full-time ministry." If that meant becoming a missionary, and ending up one day as dinner for a big snake in some jungle or rain forest, then so be it.

Within two weeks of seeing Dave for the last time, like a good businessman, I had analyzed my problem and felt I knew the answer. To put that plan in motion, however, I wanted to first speak to my dad, who had been a pastor himself for forty years. Surely, he could give me the right tips and directions I needed to make such a monumental transition. Both my twin brother and younger sister were in full-time ministry, so I expected the whole family to joyously welcome their "black sheep" businessman/son/ brother back into the fold (of sacred labor for God).

I couldn't have been more wrong.

The actual meeting with my dad was short and to the point. After listening attentively for a couple of minutes, he spoke the most perplexing wisdom I had ever heard him give. He told me to "stay in business, only serve the Lord there. If the Lord wants to move you, He'll move you."

I was stunned. In fact, I was so nonplussed by this unexpected advice that I completely forgot to ask him the obvious follow-up question: How do I do that? How do I stay in business, yet serve the Lord in my business? He had given me a skeleton of an answer, but there was no meat on those bones. From my recent experience, "serving God" and "business" seemed an utter contradiction in terms. Should I be conducting a fifteen-minute Bible study or devotional at work each morning? Or inviting my employees to church on Sunday? Or distributing gospel tracks in the entrance lobby or including them with each invoice or statement sent? Or should I offer a short prayer before company lunches? How about Christian fish bumper stickers on company vehicles? Or specialty license plates? What did serving the Lord in business mean? I contemplated that conundrum intensely for days, weeks, months, and years following that meeting with my dad.

And now, after thirty more years of contemplation, the Lord has progressively brought meat to the bones of that original answer. It is that "meat" that the Lord has laid on my heart to share with you in this book.

Looking back, I see today that serving the Lord in business is not about following a list of actions that comport with our human concepts of being a Christian, such as conducting Bible studies, distributing gospel tracks, parroting religious prayers, or trying to "witness" to all the employees. Rather, serving the Lord in business *naturally* takes place as God changes our hearts in a myriad of ways right *in* our business. Just to name a few:

- How *He* changes our *purpose* for being in business.
- How *He* changes our *view* of each employee, vendor, and customer.
- How *He* changes our *definition* of honesty and fairness.
- How *He* changes our sales and promotional *techniques.*
- How *He* makes us *sensitive* to the needs of our employees beyond their paycheck.

By God's mercy, and over decades of time, He has progressively transitioned me step-by-step to recognize an entirely different way of doing business, and doing it successfully. He has showed me *His way* of doing business. Through all of it, I have grown to recognize that God's "core business principles," what I call Kingdom Truths, are really simple and straight forward. God's way of business is dealing with all employees as His equal creations, making them feel appreciated and secure, paying a fair wage for their work, paying bills on time, saying what is true, keeping our word, and appreciating the differences in people by focusing on their strengths rather than their weaknesses. This is just a sampling of God's way for any business to become profitable and successful.

I am not saying that this book contains the only way to build a company. Far from it! But it is the path that the Lord led me to implement in growing Environment Control. I tried it my way for twenty years and I certainly was "successful," but I was destroying my life in the process. My so-called success contained no peace, no comfort, no satisfaction, and no rest. It did contain plenty of stress, anxiety, worry, and fear. There is not a shred of doubt in my mind that had God left me to my own devices in running a business, I would not be here to write this book, or to enjoy conversations with my grown children, or to sit back and delight in the growth of my grandchildren. *I'd be dead.* But, praise God! He didn't leave me to my own destructive path, and He won't leave you to falter either.

God's way is different. His path provides the wisdom to have *both* a successful business and a peaceful life. I am a grateful witness to this glorious fact. I have no doubt that you could strip out "God" from an enterprise and still make a success of it, but my experience is that God's way of business is *both* successful *and full of peace!* The core principles that are contained in this book are divine truths and they work. Put another label on them and they still work. God is God. His principles always work. If you do not believe in God, but take the time to understand and implement the principles set forth in these pages, you will experience a beneficial impact on your business. This is because God's principles, like the scientific laws of gravity or thermodynamics, are always actively at work.

For Christians, however, there is something much more profound going on. I do not know your company or the situation you find yourself. Perhaps you have a company that is steeped in political correctness and even the mention of God would be anathema to many of your employees or customers. This does not matter to God. He is able to work in your workplace just as easy as He does in mine. God is bigger than any situation you are struggling with in your business. This is particularly so because *peace in your work-place begins with peace in God's workplace—YOU!*

I will tell you from the outset that this is probably the central theme of the book. While you may think that "peace in the workplace" is all about establishing a comfortable and peaceful environment in your office workplace, God has a different perspective. The divine reality is: YOU are God's workplace. Philippians 2:13 says, "For it is God who is at work in *you*, both to will and to work for His good pleasure."

Notice the tense of this verse. God IS [presently and continually] at work in you. He is not sometimes at work in you if you live a proper life worthy of His working. He is not working in you only if you allow Him to work. Scripture makes this wonderful principle absolutely clear. God is presently, on a 24/7 continual basis, at work in you. Your business may be the worldliest enterprise you know. You may have set it up that way on purpose. It doesn't matter. Through this book you will begin a journey of en-lightenment that begins in an inward place that none can see but you. Peace in your business workplace begins with peace in God's workplace.

That workplace is your heart.

First and foremost, this is a book about *God's perspective* on business and work. This perspective is the one unfail-ing guide for successful business operations, and for that matter, everything we do in human living. It is not some kind of guarantee that your current business will be a fi-nancial success, as the world defines success (*see* chapter five, *How does God define success?*), but it means that you are going to treat people right; it means that Christ is going to be manifest through your life to the point where you will drop to your knees in your heart in awe, praise, and worship to Him, as you watch from a front row seat the power, majesty, and divine beauty of the How-Great-Thou-Art Almighty God's successful working *in you!*

The first mistake many Christians in business make is failing to put their business, and themselves, in the context of this larger perspective.

Chapter Two:

Operational Perspective

(The true environment where business operates)

> *"We know that we are of God, and that the*
> *whole world lies in the power of the evil one."*
>
> 1 JOHN 5:19

C an you remember the last time you looked through a kaleidoscope? Whether it was a cheap throw-away toy you got as a kid, something you made as a science project at school, or an expensive optical instrument you looked through in some jewelry store or museum of science, these contraptions hold curiosity and fleeting fascination for most of us. The design of these devices is usually the same: the mechanism holds bits of multi-colored glass of various shapes and sizes, held loosely at the end of a rotating tube. When the tube is held to one of the viewer's eyes, pointed at a source of light, and rotated, the viewer is rewarded with a continually changing array of colorful dancing symmetrical shapes as the light passes through the bits of glass and reflects off two or more mirrors set at angles to each other at the far end of the tube.

As fun as a *kaleidoscope* can be to idly entertain, it should never be confused with a *telescope*, which is also an optical instrument held to the viewer's eye for purpose of viewing objects with clear resolution and focus. If we want to see the world as it really is, and how we fit into that world, we need to pick up the right optical instrument. We need a telescope, not a kaleidoscope, to do so. Otherwise, our view of what we think is "reality" will actually be a dancing reflection of continual illusion.

As I briefly mentioned in the previous chapter, for the first twenty years of my life as a Christian businessman, I spent much of my time building my *own* kaleidoscope in my head, by picking up various colored bits of strategic and tactical methodologies from various newspapers and business magazines, and any number of other worldly sources. I treasured these sources as though each was a precious gem of great worth. At first, as I viewed my business and personal life through this self-made instrument, I was absorbed by what I saw dancing before me. I thought all of this was reality, but it wasn't. Not even close. After a while, even the pretty colors turned dark, and I was left with relentless patterns of fear and stress.

It wasn't until my experience at Dave's bedside, and the days immediately following, that God caused me to realize that He had already given me a *telescope*, in the form of His holy word. Shortly after my return from visiting Dave, I was asked to teach a Sunday school class on Proverbs, and I agreed. I soon sat down with *The Living Bible Paraphrased* and began to read Proverbs, just to get the overall feel for the book. I didn't get past verse two before God was putting the *telescope* to my eye and showing me reality. Proverbs 1:2–3 told me that God provided His word "to teach people how to live—how to act in *every* circumstance, for he wanted them to be understanding, just and fair in *everything* they did."

I couldn't put the book down, and by the end of that first long evening, I had read through the entire book of Proverbs several times. I realized that my whole basis for looking at things was skewed off kilter. In reality, I had approached my life and business *no differently* than any non-Christian person in the world would have approached their own business and life. I had been using a kaleido-scope rather than a telescope to view important things around me. Once I began to spend time in God's word, my world came more into focus and things grew clearer. When I relied on all of the self-help books, magazine articles, and other colorful tidbits, to view my life, I would grow con-fused, which would inevitably result in increasing fear, guilt, and stress.

When looking at any aspect of our lives, whether that is business, or employment or unemployment status, or something else, we often use the wrong optics and are either frightened or overly optimistic by what we see. We need to put aside the self-made kaleidoscope and pick up the God-made telescope. If we are to truly get a hold of our entire lives, including our jobs or businesses, we need to see the world with clear resolution and focus. For me, that clarity only comes as I turn to God's word.

Let me share with you two Kingdom Truths—one in-tensely positive and the other deeply negative—that I spent decades looking at through my self-made kaleidoscope. By doing so, neither truth came into focus for me. I was vaguely aware of the gist of each concept, but I never fully comprehended their true and important meaning, nor did I understand the implications of incalculable significance that flowed from each of them. As a result, the transforming power in each truth to dramatically alter my life was never recognized, realized, or internalized. Truths that should have been completely life-changing for me were diluted, misunderstood, and lost. I know now, that the source of all of my guilt, fear, worry, doubt, and anxiety over the years has come from my lack of fully understanding these two foundational realities. I will focus on each one briefly here, but I encourage you not to treat them lightly. May God grant all of us a deeply abiding understanding, from God's word, concerning these two foundational truths.

Foundation One: We walk on holy ground!

This one Kingdom Truth, as God progressively draws you to fully understand it, will likely revolutionize how you view your life and work forever. As Christians, we claim to understand that Jesus is the Son of God and that He lives in us. We readily acknowledge that He is God Himself and that His divine presence within us is what defines us as Christians. Look at what happened when Moses came into the presence of God. We've all read this story in Exodus 3:3–5 where Moses was attracted by the sighting of a burning bush:

> So Moses said, "I must turn aside now and see this marvelous sight, why the bush is not burned up." When the Lord saw that he turned aside to look,

God called to him from the midst of the bush and said, "Moses, Moses!" And he said, "Here I am." Then He said, "Do not come near here; remove your sandals from your feet, *for the place on which you are standing is holy ground.*"

Throughout scripture, there are places identified as *holy ground*, not because of their geographic location, but because of God's presence. God is holy and He transforms everywhere He is—into a holy place. We see this again in Joshua 5:15: "The captain of the Lord's host said to Joshua, 'Remove your sandals from your feet, for the place where you are standing is holy.' And Joshua did so." In this verse, Joshua is standing at a distance from Jericho viewing its formidable defenses. Suddenly, the Lord appeared to Joshua, as the "captain of the Lord's host," to confirm to him that God would accomplish the defeat of the city of Jericho. It was at this point that the Lord said to Joshua, "The place where you are standing *is holy.*"

Now, consider this incredible statement for a moment. Was the Lord saying to Joshua, "Hey, what a coincidence. Out of all the places your traveling has taken you in the Promised Land, you just happened to come across, and are now standing on, some ground that is holy, so take off your sandals!" Is that the meaning of this verse? Not at all! What He was saying to Joshua, which He promised him in Joshua 1:9, was that *He would be with Joshua wherever he went.* God's presence with Joshua *made the ground holy.*

If you are a Christian, this is your birthright and reality today. Wherever you are, whatever you do—because God has revealed His Son *in you,* and has promised to remain with you, direct your paths, and care for you—then wherever you are *is* holy ground. Your business or work *is* holy ground. Your home *is* holy ground. Your commute to work *is* holy ground. When you are making that sales presentation, you are standing on holy ground. When you speak to your employees or co-workers throughout the day, each time, you are on holy ground.

What makes the ground holy is not the activity you are working on at the moment; but rather, *the presence of God within you*, guiding you, caring for you, and protecting you. If you are in a business like mine, when you are cleaning that toilet, you are on holy ground. When you are polishing the floors, you are on holy ground because you have the Holy One living in you.

Perhaps you're thinking right now: *I know this already.* Then bear with me. I'll ask you two "yes or no" questions in a moment to test what you *really* know. But first, take a moment more to focus completely on this simple truth and let it sink in deeply: *Because God dwells in you; He makes your entire life holy.*

Now answer question one: Is sacred work more holy than secular work? Or to put the question another way: Is *your* work less holy than what the minister does who works down the street at the local church, or the missionary who translates the Bible into regional dialects in Africa or Asia?

This is a simple yes or no question.

If you answered yes, then you are still looking through a kaleidoscope at this foundational truth. The ground doesn't get any more holy for a person just because they happen to be employed as a full-time minister, or because they have dedicated their lives to Bible translation work as a missionary in a foreign land (as admirable as this may be). *Wherever* God dwells, *that* is holy ground. There isn't any such thing as *partially* holy ground, or *almost* holy ground, or *mostly* holy ground. The ground you are on, and the ground the full-time minister or missionary is on, is either holy or it's not holy. Only the presence of God makes the difference. The minister's God is not holier than your God. The missionary's God is not holier than your God. You are all Christians and worship the *same* God. He is the same holy God who makes the ground that you all stand on—holy! Throw out any concept that the minister's or missionary's work is more sacred and holy than your own. It's not scriptural. All are equally holy and part of God's sovereign will, because God fully lives *in* each of you.

Here's question two: Have you ever felt that God has forgotten you, or isn't listening to your prayers, or punishing you in some way, or that you are somehow not following His will for your life? If your answer is yes to any aspect of this question, I encourage you to prayerfully reconsider this fundamental truth once more.

If the *All-Knowing*, How-Great-Thou-Art Almighty God, Creator and Sustainer of the universe, lives in us continuously and forever (so that the very ground under our feet is holy), how is it that we get into our thinking that God has forgotten us, or that we have the ability or capacity to leave Him in some way? Why doesn't this notion instantly sound alarm bells in our heads as heretical and totally absurd, based on scriptural truth? It should! How can an *All-Knowing* God, a God who cannot learn (because He knows all things already), forget anything? How can God, who lives *in* us permanently, not *always* be *in* us wherever we go? This brings us squarely to the second foundational truth—that we live in a dark world filled with evil powers intent on filling our heads with lies. Satanic forces have us thinking and acting like we believe that God must be suffering from Alzheimer's or some form of dementia and can't find His way home or remember the names of His own Children. This is the view from an evil kaleidoscope if ever there was one.

But God's word—His telescope—tells every Christian the same glorious good news: You are God's dwelling place *(1 Corinthians 3:16)*. There are no qualifying considerations here. *You are God's dwelling place!* This is worthy of shouting from the rooftops. He will *never* leave you and you can *never* leave Him. Nothing can snatch you from His hands *(John 10:27-30)*. Forget all the conditional "ifs," "ands," or "buts" intruding on your thinking about God and His abode. YOU are His abode! Every conditional "if," "and," or "but" is nothing but a shattered shard of worthless colored glass slipped into your personal kaleidoscope. They are sourced not in scriptural reality, but are the seductive whispers of satanic lies spoken softly by evil forces that stalk about in pursuit of gullible prey in this present evil age.

Foundation Two: We live in a dark and evil world.

Scripture tells us "the whole world lies in the power of the evil one" *(1 John 5:19)*. This means that all of the stress and struggles we have in this life are sourced in the satanic, fallen world that we live in. Not because God is punishing us, or that He has forgotten us. Whatever difficulty you are facing now, or will face tomorrow, scripture tells us that it is because of Satan's influence throughout this world—on people's lives and throughout our culture.

Ephesians 6:12 says, "For our struggle [that means, what I am worrying about at this moment, what I'm stressed over, what I'm tempted to be angry about, what I'm disappointed in] is not against flesh and blood [that is, against people], but against the rulers, against the powers, against the world forces of this darkness, against the spiritual forces of wickedness in the heavenly places." *The Living Bible Paraphrased* makes this verse even clearer, "For we are not fighting against people made of flesh and blood, but against persons without bodies—the evil rulers of the unseen world, those mighty satanic beings and great evil princes of darkness who rule this world; and against huge numbers of wicked spirits in the spirit world."

This is our true source of struggle. It is a struggle against forces that hunger to make us miserable, angry, selfish, and self-centered. It is a struggle that affects God's own people. We are not immune from it. Ignoring this truth, or subtly trying to minimize or marginalize it, only places us at greater disadvantage. I imagine that Satan and his minions laugh at our blind naiveté. Yes, we understand that prior to God revealing His Son in us, we all lived exclusively in this dark and evil world. But as Christians, we read that God has "rescued us from the domain of darkness and transferred us to the kingdom of His beloved Son" *(Colossians 1:13)*. We understand from this verse that there are two kingdoms, or two worlds full of activity, and God has *removed* us from one (the kingdom of darkness) and put us in the other (the kingdom of light). Doesn't that mean we are no longer affected by the kingdom of darkness? *Far from it!*

God's enemy is a master of allusion, aspersion, nuance, and misdirection. The very air he breathes is innuendo, implication, intimation, and insinuation. He relishes in the bold audacity of misdirecting our thinking away from the awareness that this is a present evil age, to a demented place where we question or blame our own Heavenly Father, the true source of our life and everything we possess in this world. From the seed of this evil lie, which yields fruit only in the soil of profound spiritual ignorance, comes the fruit of self-centered human thought: *Hey, I just got laid off from work (or my business is failing no matter how much I pray; or my spouse is really sick), and I don't understand what I've done to displease God, or why He's not blessing me.* The same old trick used on Adam and Eve still works on us.

I will discuss "God's blessing" in a future chapter. But for now, I want to focus on the fact that just because God has rescued us from the *domain of darkness*, doesn't mean that He has *removed* us from it. We certainly are no longer a citizen *of* the kingdom of darkness, but we still live *in* it. Listen in on a prayer from Jesus to the Father, recorded in John 17:11, 14–17:

> I [Jesus] am no longer *in* the world; and *yet they them-selves [disciples] are **in** the world*, and I come to You ... I have given them Your word; and the world has hated them, because they are not *of* the world, even as I am not *of* the world. ***I do not ask You to take them out of the world***, but to keep them from the evil one. They are not *of* the world, even as I am not *of* the world. Sanctify them in the truth; *Your word is truth.*

Scripture tells us that we are not *of* the world, but we still live *in* it. This means that the struggle mentioned in

Ephesians 6:12 is our struggle. Christians are not immune to it and it seems as though these demonic powers focus with particular zeal their activities on God's own children. This can get confusing if we try to make sense of it through our own kaleidoscopic human logic. But think of it this way: Picture in your mind two worlds full of events and activities going on at the same time. One is the lesser, dark, earthly world, and the other is God's greater, heavenly kingdom of light. The lesser earthly world is the realm where we physically live out our lives even though we have the heavenly kingdom living within us. Scripture tells us that Satan utterly controls this lesser earthly kingdom. The Holy Spirit is certainly a mitigating force within it, but Satan is allowed to rule in it during this age.

In this dark world, evil touches equally the lives of every man, woman, and child, whether they are God's children or Satan's progeny. The greatest evidence of this is that we all die. No one can dispute the fact that the sun rises on the evil and the good and it rains on the righteous and the unrighteous *(Matthew 5:45)*. However, the evil that animates the bad things that happen in this world is *not* random, and it is not fair or unbiased; it has a purpose, and it has a source.

Satan has always been committed to frustrate God's eternal plan *(Genesis 3:1–7)*, snatch God's word of His kingdom away from hearts too hard to receive it *(Mark 4:15)*, divert Jesus from His redemptive mission through his temptations *(Matthew 4:1–11; Mark 1:12–13; Luke 4:1–13)*, deceive Jesus through Peter *(Mark 8:33)*, betray Jesus through Judas *(Luke 22:3)*, lay hands on the Lord's disciples and sift them like chaff *(Luke 22:31)*, and in this modern era, distract us from God's continual work in us *(Philippians 2:13)* to transform us from glory to glory into His Son's image *(2 Corinthians 3:18)*.

Bottom line to understand, here, is that we cannot take evil out of this world—it is the home of evil because God has confined evil to this realm alone. God allows no preference between the just and the unjust because this is the means by which, in His sovereign wisdom, He glorifies His Son in the midst of this dark place.

This situation was graphically described by Jesus in the parable of the wheat and the tares *(Matthew 13:24–30, 36–43)*. The enemy of God has sown tares among God's wheat field, and God has decided to allow both the tares and the wheat to grow together until the harvest at the end of the age. So, like it or not, the world is a polluted field that we must live in and endure.

Of course, God knows every dark detail in this world that Satan controls, and He obviously does *allow* some negative things to happen to us. It is not for us to understand every detail or reason why He allows these things (although, I will discuss God's most basic reason in the next chapter). What He has granted to our understanding is His promise to work it all together for our good *(Romans 8:28)*. We may not see the *good* that God works for us *immediately* upon experiencing the bad, but we are assured from scripture that God is working all of these things together for our good. That is the *ultimate* difference between God's children and those who live in this world without hope.

God never promised that *our businesses* would take care of us, or *our employers* would be fair to us. *God promised that HE would take care of us.* To be sure, God may, for a time in our lives, provide income we need through a particular business or job. If we become unemployed, He might provide some of what we need for a period of time through government assistance (which we paid into while working), or our church, or other Christian friends. Or He might lead us to move to another community and take up an entirely different occupation.

Sometimes God's provision comes in a way or in a form that we simply do not understand. Like Israel in the desert, God may provide "manna from heaven" to care for us. *Manna* is a funny word that explains our situation perfectly at times. We see in Exodus 16:15, as the children of Israel were crossing the desert with nothing to eat, God sent them manna. This Hebrew word "manna" means "what is it?" (*mān = what; hû' = is it?*). Sometimes God provides for us in ways that we can't begin to explain, let alone understand.

Doing business in a battle zone.
Now, let's use these two foundational truths to gain insight into our work or business. Let's say God calls you to start a business and you want to run it properly to honor Him. The above principle related to evil should make it clear that no amount of prayer will ever *totally* separate or insulate your business from the influences prevalent in this world. When you experience hard times, it has nothing to do with God's displeasure or lack of blessing. It has nothing to do with the fact that you have abandoned your position on holy ground. That is just the way evil is—it wants to distract you from God; it wants to get that kaleidoscope up to your eye and get you focused on yourself. We are constantly in a battle against evil influences.

To the extent that you are building a business, you do build it on holy ground because Christ lives in you. He causes you to worship Him, and to talk to Him; and He communicates with you. But that doesn't make the customers you service righteous, or their motives pure. It doesn't make vendors dependable, or the government efficient, or your employees reliable. Nothing guarantees that you are going to be dealt with justly because you live on holy ground; or that someone won't steal from you; or sue you; or how the economy will impact your revenue.

That's why I like to keep the reality of these two opposing worlds fresh in my consciousness all the time. There is a kingdom of light and a kingdom of darkness. Look how Paul described it in 2 Corinthians 4:6–10:

> For God, who said, "Light shall shine out of darkness," is the One who has shone in our hearts to give the Light of the knowledge of the glory of God in the face of Christ. **But we have this treasure in earthen vessels**, so that the surpassing greatness of the power will be of God and not from ourselves; we are **afflicted in every way**, *but not crushed*; **perplexed**, but *not despairing*; **persecuted**, *but not forsaken*; **struck down**, *but not destroyed*; always carrying about in the body the dying of Jesus, so that the life of Jesus also may be manifested in our body (emphasis added).

We see two worlds in brutal combat in these verses. As long as we live in this dark world we will be **afflicted in every way**, **perplexed**, **persecuted**, and **struck down**; BUT we will never be *crushed*, *forsaken*, or *destroyed* because we have the Greater One in us. The Apostle John says, "Greater is He who is in you than he who is in the world" *(1 John 4:4)*. When we see our world environment, as John and Paul saw it, then we will never *despair* regardless of the circumstances surrounding us. *We are of the kingdom of light and are on holy ground;* we have the Greater One in us, working all things together for our good.

Chapter Three:

Transformational Perspective

(God's *singular* goal for our lives)

*"Upon You I was cast from birth; You have
been my God from my mother's womb."*

PSALM 22:10

W hy God has kept me in a business that I didn't want to stay in—I don't claim to fully under-stand. Why this business has survived five major recessions—I don't know. It isn't any greater bless-ing on my life than it is on all of the thousands of other employees who work at the EC family of companies. The answers to these questions are within the heart and mind of God and are far beyond our ability to understand, let alone define and explain in this book.

I can only say that God knows us, through and through. He knows every aspect of who we are and how we are made. On the positive side, He knows our God-given talents and intellect, our capacity to analyze data and be flexible, and our social and leadership skills. He also knows our darker side: that within us dwell pride, selfish desires, and fleshly propensities. For example, as I mentioned before, He knew before I was born that I would be obsessively attracted to making money. My wife, by contrast, isn't attracted to making money at all. God knew this as well. He knew that once I got a taste for making money, it would trigger a hunger in my flesh to compulsively fret over making *more* money. God knew that money was a false god in my heart and that I trusted in money more than I trusted in Him. In His sovereignty, He didn't allow this false trust to remain dormant in my heart. He placed me in a work situation precisely suited to activate, and then progressively kill, this false god. He knew the misery it would bring me. In His love and mercy, He desired that I be freed from its claim.

A lot of people end up owning their own businesses for all kinds of good (and not-so-good) reasons. Most begin their businesses with the best of intentions. They need income to support their families, or they enjoy working with people and have the personal skills and an entrepreneurial disposition to be their own bosses. Other people may have no desire at all to be in business for themselves, but rather, are satisfied to be considered faithful and loyal employees. Whatever the initial reason or motivation, their working environment may suit the talents and skills given to them by God, but also might stir up deeper elements of pride, greed, and competitiveness that they didn't know they had.

I'm not judging anybody's motivation for getting into business. Frankly, why we initially find ourselves in business is not really relevant. My point here is that we are all different. We are all animated by different motivations. Not everyone ends up in their own business. Not everyone *wants* to be in their own business. Not everyone *should* be in their own business. But all of this variety is part of God's allowance and will over all of our lives. Whether we know it, or acknowledge it, God is already at work in our lives, even from our mother's womb *(Psalm 22:10)*, to accomplish His good pleasure in us.

God's singular purpose for all of His children.
From God's perspective there is only one thing in common among all of us. That commonality is centered in *what God is accomplishing in us* as we work and live our lives. Philippians 1:6 says, "For I [the Apostle Paul is speaking here] am confident of this very thing, that He who began a good work in you will perfect it until the day of Christ Jesus." The main purpose of that good work in every person, no matter the infinitude of their differences, is to conform them to the image of His Son *(Romans 8:29)*. He does this conforming work in each of us by drawing us to *fully trust in Him*. That's the main purpose of His work in us.

He will bring each of us into the singularity of His purpose—to trust Him in *everything*—as He progressively conforms our life to Christ's life in us. Is this a process that we can jot down on our "to do" list each morning to accomplish? No. This is God's work. As Paul declared in Galatians 2:20, "I have been crucified with Christ; and it is no longer I who live, but Christ lives in me; and the life which I now live in the flesh I live by faith [that is, by trusting] in the Son of God, who loved me and gave Himself up for me." Are we the "light of the world" or "the salt of the earth" on our own? Again, the answer is no. But Christ is the killing salt and disinfecting light in us, as He brings those attributes of His life progressively into our lives as we trust His working in us.

During our temporal, very short journey on earth, He ordains that we work and He directs us into the work He would have us do. This work may be temporary or permanent. As we live our lives, this work may change from time to time, according to His will. Many of us find ourselves employed in a particular position for two years, and then unbeknownst to us, we find ourselves facing a job change. This change may constitute a move, or it may mean a switch of careers. Some of us find ourselves out of work for a period of time, or led to set up our own businesses for income. Some of us find ourselves in our own businesses for the duration of our lives, while others own businesses for a while and then due to economic conditions, or whatever, find themselves out of business and looking for work once more. Through all of these transitional events, God is faithfully working to bring us to a place where we trust Him for everything in our lives—whatever comes our way.

My own personal testimony is that the power of God's grace changed me from wanting to make more and more money to just praising Him. Another dear brother I know has been out of work for two years. Yet another is in business, but his income has dropped in half because of the economy. God is bringing all of us to the same place—*to trust Him*. You can try to resist it and wish that you had more ability or faith, but God is *still* God. He has guaranteed to perfect His working in you until the day of Christ Jesus. And He is working to bring us all to this same place of trusting Him for everything. I think this really clarifies for the believer what is actually going on in this life. It brings us to the essence and central point of our walk as Christians: that we walk on holy ground, trusting God step by step for everything, because He *is* taking care of us.

Perhaps you're thinking, *I already trust Him for everything, or at least most things. I pray to Him for just about everything. He just doesn't answer my prayers sometimes.*

Let me ask you a question: If God promised to give you one or the other, would you take a million dollars cash or more faith?

You choose.

Two workplaces.
God knew that I would get into a business that I didn't want to be in, but found myself owning and operating anyway. He knew that I did so with the good motivation to provide for my growing family. Yet, at the same time, He used this same business workplace to expose my hidden love for the false god of money. Another man may be unemployed and struggling over his temporary inability to bring in sufficient income to support his family. He has a strong motivation to work, and works hard every day to find a job, yet he remains out of work for a time. God knows this too, and even in such times of hardship, while this man perseveres in the hard task of finding a job, God is *also working* to strengthen this man's faith. Each of us could add a dozen more examples to these two. The point is: God is using all of our life-experiences to renew our minds and draw us into a deeper trust in Him, the one true provider of

everything we need. He knows we are incapable of doing this on our own.

I find this easiest to understand by thinking of an analogy of two different workplaces. One of these workplaces we all know really well; the other we may know less well. Yet, both are critical to transforming our lives into a "place" that fosters peace and contentment, regardless of our outward circumstances. Of course, God is sovereign Lord over *both* of these workplaces, but it often helps me to understand this spiritual truth with greater clarity if I consider it from two different "workplace" perspectives.

The first "workplace" is *our workplace*: it is our life as it unfolds before us day-by-day and year-by-year. We labor in this workplace and experience all of the joys and sorrows that it yields. If you are currently employed, or have a business, this workplace includes your work or business environment. In this sense, it is the office, store, warehouse, or work site you go to each day. It is the place that we think a lot about and worry over. It is the source of great satisfaction when things are going well—and a great deal of stress and anxiety when they are not. It is the place that often competes for the time our families would otherwise like to share with us, particularly so, if we view it as the *only* source of the income that provides food, clothing, housing, and security for them. For many, this workplace is nothing special, and is perhaps more drudgery than pleasure. It is a means to an end. We may not be excited about it, but if we didn't have this work, what would we do? How would we provide for our families?

The second "workplace" is *God's workplace*: the one that lies within our hearts and minds. It is the workplace that Philippians 2:13 refers to when it declares: "For it is God who is [present tense] at work *in* you, both to will and to work for His good pleasure." As we can see from Philippians 2:13, God is diligently performing His work *in us* to His satisfaction (that is, to "His good pleasure"). The verse uses the *present* verb tense to describe God's working. Using the present tense assures us that it is *ongoing and continuous* without stopping—that is to say, the 24/7 working of God. Scripture also alludes to the fact that this workplace is God's "work of art." In Ephesians 2:10, the Greek word for "workmanship" is ποίημα (poiēma) which is the same word that we derive our English word: poem.

Most of this book gives focus to various aspects of this second workplace, so I will not spend more time describing it here. The important thing to note about it, though, is the fact that it is *God's workplace*. This may sound simplistic, even infantile, but it has profound implications and consequence to our living as Christians. I'll use my own experience, here, to describe what I mean.

In my earlier years, I worked hard in my business workplace. I also prayed hard for God to bless this business, but He often felt distant and aloof to me, perhaps even uninterested. I saw His hand in my life from time to time, but as a general rule, God was predominantly "out of sync" with my urgent needs (as I perceived them) and the "proper" timing (meaning my preferred timing) for satisfying those needs. This feeling often led me to conclude that I had displeased God in some way, which drove me to dedicate and rededicate myself to Him in a never-ending cycle of repentance. I attempted to live the "victorious Christian life" at a relentless pace, to the point of deep exhaustion, and physical and mental ill-health. I felt frustrated, anxious, and trapped.

It never occurred to me that God was actually not distant at all, but was intimately close, and busy working in His workplace; that is, in the gentle process of renewing my heart and mind with Himself. It never occurred to me that the countless places in scripture—all attributing God's workplace solely to His working—actually meant what they said. I was still bound with preconceived notions about God and what it meant to please Him, to cooperate and partner with Him, as a tireless and faithful disciple.

Now I recognize the duality of these two workplaces, and this realization produces great peace within me. When I pray to God concerning a certain matter, and He appears silent, I no longer see this as a warning sign that my relationship with Him is on thin ice. Rather, it tells me that He is calling me to trust Him for *everything*, even the thing that I so fervently prayed for. I can enter His rest, knowing that all His ways are peace *(Proverbs 3:17)*. I now realize that God's so-called "silence" is really His answer directing me to *wait* for further guidance. Just because He doesn't direct us into action at the very moment we pray does not mean He is ignoring us. What it actually means is that: (i) He is working to answer our prayers according to His good purpose for us, and (ii) He simply isn't directing us to take a particular action at that moment. Some things take time to work through. I now know that He is *always working* in His workplace—the workplace of my heart—to accomplish what is best for my ultimate good, and for "His good pleasure."

We are finite and God is infinite. We go to our work-places and put in eight to ten hours in a day and need to go home to rest. God is working in His workplace 24 hours a day, seven days a week, 365 days a year. Knowing this really takes the stress off my relationship with God.

Chapter Four:

Contextual Perspective

(A broader view of security and happiness)

> *"And who of you by being worried*
> *can add a single hour to his life?"*
> MATTHEW 6:27

We live in a world that screams at us every day: We *need* a number of earthly things to be happy. We *need* enough money, we *need* good health, we *need* a successful career, we *need* a couple of good looking kids, we *need* a growing retirement account, and we *need* a certain amount of pleasure/fun. Because we are constantly bombarded with this mantra, even as Christians, we tend to buy into it. We work feverishly to attain these so-called necessities, and anything that frustrates, inhibits, threatens, or prevents our attainment of any of them, is the source of great unhappiness, dissatisfaction, and stress. It does not take long for us to wonder why God isn't blessing us, which is founded on the fearful thought that He may actually be mad at us, or actively punishing us in some way for not being a "good enough" Christian. We are soon convinced that we must be "out of God's will," and a deeper worry sets in.

God's plan for believers, however, is entirely different. He is the How-Great-Thou-Art Almighty God, and we are His children. His plan is not based on our *effort*, but on His *family*. We are the kids *He has chosen* to live in His house. All of us manage to stir up a fair amount of trouble for ourselves during our "growing up" lives, but we still live in *His* house. We are still *His* kids and *He* has promised that we will never lack for any *good thing* because *He is our Father. He* will provide for us—even miraculously—those things that are *good* for us.

This does not necessarily mean that what *we think* is "good" for us is the same thing as what *God knows* is good for us. Remember, we're just kids. Some of us want the sparkly versions of all the toys mentioned in the first paragraph. We are convinced that bigger, newer, and more is better. Bigger houses, newer cars, higher incomes, deeper diversity in our investment portfolios and retirement accounts, and a relentlessly successful business enterprise will be "just the ticket" to create stability and security in our lives. These are the things we think of as God's blessings.

Others of us kids are more introspective and less grandiose. We don't mind putting in a fair day's work, even working hard at times, but should it really be *this* hard? We're not stupid—we've read about Dad's promises to bless us. Well then, we want our blessings now, and we want it set on automatic pilot for delivery throughout our lives at a level of ever-increasing abundance. And when we need more, or something specific, we want it delivered *how* we want it, in the *manner* in which we want it, and in the precise *timing* that we want it. Short of that, we think there must be a problem. Dad must be mad at us for something. "Hello up there! I've just lost my job!" or "Can you hear me? My business is NOT doing well!" Maybe He has forgotten us or is punishing us in some way. Again, our bottom-line measurement for God's blessing is how many items we've acquired from the list in the first paragraph. We certainly don't need all the sparkle that others strive for, but we want our blessings delivered on time and as ordered.

Fortunately for us kids, God is the adult in the room. He is the loving and faithful parent who knows what is *really good* for us, and has purposed to bring all of His good pleasure for us into reality in our lives. He knows that what we spend our lives chasing actually provides little security at all. He knows that in the blink of an eye, any or all of those things listed above can be wiped clean away—that they represent only a 3D holographic illusion of security and safety. Because He is our Father, He knows what *true security* is, and where it is found. He knows that it is not found in the many things that this world claims to be necessary for happiness and security. Our security, thank God, has nothing to do with us. It has everything to do with Him—our great and loving God, living *within us*.

The ultimate Kingdom Truth.

Before we get further along in this, I want to share with you what I think is *the* ultimate Kingdom Truth. It is a foundational principle that far exceeds anything else I could possibly share with you about the operation of a business.

It applies to everyone equally, whether employed, unemployed, or self-employed; whether you are wealthy, poor, or recently bankrupt; a new hire, tenured manager, or the owner of a company. If you understand this one core principle, you understand the entire book, and I will consider my task complete. You will find this Kingdom Truth in the ninth verse of Proverbs 16:

> **The mind of man plans his way,**
> **But the Lord directs his steps.**

I am a living testimony to this abiding truth. When I started Environment Control fifty years ago, I firmly believed that I was doing so only to provide enough income to pay a few bills and get through college. *That was my human plan.* I fully intended to sell it as soon as I graduated. I didn't know then that I would still be in this same business fifty years later:

- *Five years into the business:* There was *no way* I would stay.
- *Ten years into the business:* I was *still looking* for ways out.
- *Twenty years into the business:* I *continued to search* for something else to do.

So, I'm still here. I can't honestly tell you that I planned it, or that I have ever wanted to be in it. In fact, I can't take credit for any of it. But I can share what I've learned from it, beginning with this: I'm currently in this business after fifty years because this is where the Lord has directed *me* to be *for the present time.* It certainly has never been my plan, but it has been God's sovereign hand in my life. He has been my God from my mother's womb *(Psalm 22:9-10).* He has directed my paths in the way He would have me go *(Proverbs 3:6, NKJV).*

Over these fifty years, the business has endured five major recessions and could have lost everything in any one of them. But it hasn't. Is this because I'm such a great businessman? No way! There are plenty of good Christian businessmen and women who found themselves unemployed, or forced out of business, during this same period of time. Did that happen to them because God was punishing them, cursing them, withholding blessings from them, or some such thing? Again, no way! God was simply directing their paths out of the businesses they were presently in, just as He was keeping me *in* a business that for approximately the first twenty-five years *I didn't want to be a part of.*

Let me share with you a lunch I recently had with another Christian businessman. It's just one of hundreds of such lunches I've had over the years. After a few pleasantries, my lunch companion launched straight into what concerned him. His head and heart were a blur of anxiety about his business:

"Daryl, I'm really agonizing over my business. No matter what I do, revenues keep declining. I keep praying, and I read in scripture where God promises to bless me, but I don't know why I'm not experiencing His blessing."

I said, "You are."

He said, "What do you mean?"

I said, "God's blessing is on *your life.* It's what God promises to do *in* and *through* your life from the moment He put you in Christ and Christ in you. He has promised to care for you in everything."

"Yeah, but what about my business?"

I said, "Someday, you are going to look back on this time of worry, as I do now on a time when a friend and colleague of mine sued me, and you are going to praise and worship God for His loving protection, provision, direction, and care in your life during this time. I don't know what that means for you or your current business right now, but I do know God is directing and caring for you.

"I'll tell you what happened to me during that lawsuit. I was angry and upset: with my colleague, myself, and with God. In my view, it was a totally bogus and unjust legal action, but I still had to borrow money to settle it. Why did the Lord allow this to happen? How would I survive the financial burden? My mind was flooded with the same worries that are running through your head right now. But today, I wouldn't trade the $20,000 it cost me to settle that litigation if somebody offered me $200,000 for the experiences and sensitivity I gained from it.

"God showed me, over subsequent years, a number of things about myself that were sourced in the insights I received as a result of that civil complaint. The inward sensitivity that now comes as second nature to me, when speaking to employees, stems from that legal action of decades earlier. He knew back then, when my sales were $250,000 a year, that today I would be responsible for a franchise organization which services franchises across the country that have annual sales in excess of seventy million a year. He taught me lessons early on, that today I consider priceless. I can look back now and see how God was working *within me* to reveal:

- My pride at having to win at everything.
- My lack of trust in Him to care for me when people were treating me wrong (Psalm 103:6).

- How the legal system in America really works; how easy it is to find yourself facing a discrimination charge even though you don't discriminate; how easy it is for a disgruntled employee to find a hungry lawyer advertising on some late night television program, and to file a lawsuit without cause.
- How I live in a world that isn't just or fair.
- He was teaching me the importance of faithfully practicing something as simple as writing down important discussions; never leaving any important conversation or meeting to a "He said–I said" verbal scenario later on.

"I could go on and on. I didn't know it at the time, but God was working *in me* on all of these fronts. He was not satisfied with only growing my trust in Him spiritually. He was also orchestrating a far bigger personal growth program for my benefit. He was preparing my reservoir of personal experiences and business skills, in practical terms, to meet the challenges of what He knew I would need for the next fifty years—all of which I had absolutely no clue about in those early days."

My lunch companion sat quietly for a moment, considering his next question. Then he asked, "What if your business had been destroyed because of that lawsuit, would that have been God's 'blessing' on you? That would be a strange way of providing for you, don't you think?"

Putting your work into context.
"Brother," I said, "You need to put your current business, or any job you have in the future, into the *context of your entire life.* Your life is much more important to God than

your business. God has promised to bless *your life* and He will never fail you in this promise. From what I now know, after fifty years of business, I'm inclined to think that it really is immaterial as to what career we find ourselves in, not that God doesn't lead us, but the real focus of God's work is *in our life*.

"But I'll give you an answer to your question: I wouldn't have said that the failure of my business must be God's curse. I wouldn't have said that it's because I failed God. I wouldn't have said, in any way, shape, or form, that God isn't blessing me. I would have said, based on my under-standing today, that businesses fail, people lose their jobs, people come down with cancer, children are abused, loved ones are injured (or killed) in car accidents, all because this is a broken world we live in. It's not the perfect environ-ment that God created, but the malicious, malignant, and malevolent cesspool of iniquity caused by Adam's fall and Satan's industry.

"God has never promised the Christian in business: to bless their business with ever-higher revenues and per-sonal income from now until they go to glory without interruption, just because they are Christian. They are no better, or special, than anyone else in this regard; and they certainly are no worse. They simply are people who find themselves in business as part of God's direction in their life. It isn't necessarily permanent. I could have easily had two or three (or more) jobs over the same period of time. That's the experience of probably the majority of people. As God directs our lives, we need not hold onto our work or business with too tight a grasp. What fifty years of being in business tells me, then, is that it was God's will to use the *Environment Control* business: not only in my life, but in the lives of scores of franchisees, and in the lives of tens of thousands of employees, vendors, and customers over those fifty years."

Again, my lunch partner paused and took a moment to rub his eyes to ward off the tiredness I could see in them. It was clear that our lunch conversation wasn't going the way he had anticipated. I could tell that he was mulling over another question, but didn't quite know how to phrase it. I took another bite of lunch, not wanting to rush him. Finally, he asked his next question this way:

"Okay, Daryl, let's say I accept what you're saying as true, which I'm not sure I do, but let's say I do for purposes of this question. If what you say is true, then it can *only* be true if I am following God's will for my life. What you are saying is great, even glorious, *as long as* I am being obedient to God. The 'fly in my soup,' Daryl, is the fact that I haven't always been obedient to God; I haven't always followed God's will. You may have figured out how to do that, but I haven't. I'm a monumental disappointment to God. To be honest with you, I don't even know what His will is for me half the time, let alone follow it."

I smiled warmly at this dear brother and nodded. Now we were getting to the crux of the matter, and his thinking was tracking exactly my logic from so many years before.

"That's a good and honest question," I said, "In fact, it's a fantastic question because when you hear God's answer you're going to be dancing around this restaurant in joy and praise to Him. Based on your last comment, let me take the rest of this lunch and share with you how it is *impossible to disappoint God*. Then we'll schedule another lunch for next week and I'll share with you that it is *impossible to be out of God's will for your life*. Would that answer two big questions for you?"

My companion's eyebrows shot up and he could only nod his willingness to listen.

"Great, I'll take that as a yes. But first, we need to touch on one preliminary truth. What you asked makes logical sense from our human perspective. But Isaiah 55:8 says that God's ways are not our ways and our thoughts are not His thoughts. That's the *first* big statement I want you to think about. Take a moment to let it sink in."

I took another bite of lunch and chewed slowly.

Then I continued.

It is impossible to disappoint God!

"The truth, from God's perspective, is that He knows everything about us already: every right and wrong choice we would ever make, every sin we would ever commit, including the ones we haven't lived long enough to commit yet. He knew about all of this stuff before we were ever born. Scripture says that He knew it all before the foundation of the world. But we so often get caught up in our own ego-centric world of worries that we forget He's omniscient, or what we call All-knowing. All-knowing means, in practical terms, that He can't be surprised. And if He can't be surprised, then He can't be disappointed. That's the *second* big statement I want you to let sink in for a moment!"

I took another bite of lunch.

"He can't 'learn' because He already knows everything. The same goes for our human concept of disappointment. When we try to lay that human attribute on the All-knowing

God it just doesn't work. It is impossible for Him to be disappointed because He already knows everything. Our human mind thinks that He must be expecting us to do one thing, while we 'surprise' Him by doing something else. We are certain that this 'disappoints Him' and we have 'let Him down' by our conduct. But this is not possible when we are talking about God. *We can never surprise Him or let Him down in this way.* I know this may seem obvious, once you think about it, but many people never think about it. They jump immediately to the human conclusion that they must be a disappointment to God. It is a conclusion that is diametrically opposed to the nature of God.

"The reality is much different and far more positive: ***It was God who, knowing everything about you before the foundation of the world, was the One who chose you to be His child!*** Scripture is quite clear: You didn't choose God, *He chose you from before the foundation of the world (Ephesians 1:4)*! Does that sound like you are a disappointment to Him? Not at all! In truth, we are a joy and pleasure to Him. We are His *workmanship (Ephesians 2:10)*.

"Our fears of disappointing God are completely unscriptural. They run contrary to the attributes of God. Consequently, they are the source of much needless stress and worry in our lives. Unfortunately, we often project onto God our own limited human frailties and attributes: our finite lack of understanding and knowledge, our false expectations about other people, our surprise when those expectations are not met, and ultimately, our disappointment.

"But these are not God's thoughts, nor are they His ways. They have nothing to do with God's divine attributes. He knows *all things* and therefore has no need to harbor expectations, is *never* surprised, and is *never* disappointed. And while we're on the topic of 'never,' let me add one more: He *never* fails. He is the How-Great-Thou-Art Almighty God. He already knows *everything* about you. And He has made you an unequivocal promise: He is going to direct your life according to *His will*, and accomplish *His will* in your life. There is nothing more absolute or secure than that.

"Look at Isaiah 46:9–10, where God makes this clear: 'My purpose will be established, and I will accomplish all *My* good pleasure.' I ask you, how emphatic and inclusive has God made this? Is any part of what God intends for your life *excluded* from that absolute statement?"

My lunch companion was getting interested now, "No, that's clear enough," he said.

"'My purpose *will* be established, and I *will* accomplish *all* my good pleasure.'" I repeated the verse again with an emphasis on the absolutes in the verse. "Does it say, 'I expect you to accomplish my good pleasure, so be faithful, willing, and diligent to do so at all times … and don't disappoint me!'? No, God spoke an absolute truth about what He *personally* has promised to do: '*I will* accomplish *all* MY good pleasure.'"

By the end of our lunch together, my companion didn't break out in dancing around the restaurant, but he was clearly beginning to see two critical Kingdom Truths. He was looking at his business in its right perspective, within the broader *context of his entire life*; and He was coming to grips with the mind-blowing freedom that comes from realizing that he could *never disappoint God*. Of course, he couldn't wait for our next lunch to learn the next Kingdom Truth: that it is *impossible to be out of God's* **WILL** *for your life.*

We met again in a couple of weeks and had that follow-up conversation about this next Kingdom Truth (which I will share with you in a moment in the context of another conversation I had with an artist friend of mine). By then, he was starting to appreciate the fact that what God promises, He keeps. After all, even from our human perspective, when we give someone our personal promise, do we expect someone else to keep that promise for us? Certainly not! We know the value of keeping our word.

So does God.

In truth, we have been "unemployed"—by God—from all of our self-effort. We have been freed to simply *rest* in the *divine peace* that He causes to abide in us. I think we can all testify to the fact (from our own experiences) that "divine peace" is nothing that can be fabricated in our own effort. *Trusting* God during our lives, and in so many situations at work and in business, is the same way. I once thought the definition of "trust" was that I needed to do a certain action, and if that action was based on my trust in God, then God would respond with a reciprocal action. It was a kind of *cause and effect* formula. But now I see this divine truth more clearly. In reality we can't manufacture the *trust* we need on our own. God is the only source of this progressive life-flow of *trust* in us. Like Christ's declaration in John 15:1–5 that He is the Vine and we are the branches, God supplies trust from the Vine to the branch, and every other thing we need each and every day of our lives, as He accomplishes *all* of His good pleasure within us. The more we see the truth of God's good news gospel, the more we find ourselves dropping to our knees in our hearts in praise and worship to Him: For God has done it all...He is all we need!

No matter where you find yourself—in an unjust divorce, or an economy taking a toll on your business or costing you your job, or dealing with a rebellious child—no matter where you find yourself, it is not a surprise to God. He hasn't forgotten you. He knew you would be facing these challenges from before the foundation of the world, yet He still chose you to be His child. And as your Father, He has set a path of *divine peace* for you throughout every single day of your life, and has prepared ways for you to travel, and lessons and skills for you to learn and acquire, that you cannot possibly recognize or realize now; but in time, you will praise Him for it for the rest of your life.

"Faithful is He who calls you, and He also will bring it to pass" *(1 Thessalonians 5:24).*

"Oh, the depth of the riches both of the wisdom and knowledge of God! How unsearchable are His judgments and unfathomable His ways!" *(Romans 11:33).*

It is impossible to be out of God's will.

Now, let me share the conversation I had with my artist friend. I met with him recently because he was stressing over what God wanted him to do with his life. In my view, he was a very talented and highly accomplished artist who was successfully supporting his family through the sale of his art. Obviously, God had endowed him with a significant gift, but he was agonizing over whether he was doing the right thing. Would he be able to support his family in five years from now on his art alone? Was he working hard enough? Did God want him to do this for the rest of his life?

I said, "Here's the good, good, good news of God. Are you ready? You don't need to know the answers to any of those questions. Just walk away from all of it."

He looked at me with a blank stare.

"Let me explain what I mean by that. God *is* (present tense) at work in you. Twenty years from now you will see this more clearly than you do now (Proverbs 4:18). Forty years from now you will see even more clearly than you will in twenty years. God is directing your steps. He has been directing your steps, from conception in your mother's womb, right up to today. He has directed your steps into this fellowship so we could look at some verses and I could share with you my own experience. And then God will take His living word from scripture and His speaking in your heart, and couple it with my testimony, and integrate that into your experience and life. Over time, He will continue to polish the truth revealed in these verses, as new circumstances enter your life, and He directs your path further. Will you be selling your art for a living in five years? I don't know, only God knows. How will you be supporting your family in five years? Only God knows.

"Here are three verses for you to consider. The *first* is Psalm 37:23, which tells us, 'The steps of a man are *established* by the LORD, and He *delights* in his way.' Jeremiah 29:11 is the *second* verse and provides a further word of comfort from the Lord, 'For I know the plans that I have for you.' The *third* verse is Proverbs 20:24 (TLB) and is the clincher for clarifying how much we must understand about God's leading: 'Since the Lord is directing our steps, why try to understand everything that happens along the way?'

"This is why Paul expressed confidence when he declared in Philippians 1:6, 'I am *confident* of this very thing, that He who began a good work in you *will* perfect it until the day of Christ Jesus.' This assurance is given repeatedly throughout scripture (*Job 42:2; Psalm 22:9–10; John 4:14; Romans 4:4–6, 8:29–39; 1 Corinthians 1:30; 2 Corinthians 3:3–5, 18, 9:8; Galatians 3:3; Philippians 2:13; 1 Thessalonians 2:13; Hebrews 13:21*).

"I tell business people, because I have been in business: I don't know for sure what I'll be doing a year from now, five years from now, or what my business will be doing in five years. The one thing I do know is that God *will accomplish* His purpose in my life."

My companion was not entirely buying this notion that God will accomplish His will in his life without any effort on his part. He said, "Yeah, that's fine for you, Daryl, you've made your money already. What about those of us who survive hand to mouth?"

I said, "This has nothing to do with how much money we are making at the time. You could be making $25,000 a year or one million dollars a year; it doesn't matter. God will accomplish His will in your life. And He will do so in ways that are different from your ways. That means there is no point trying to help Him with His task. He may allow something into your life that changes the trajectory of your entire life that you do not see now. This is the raw truth about God and His sovereignty in our lives. In the final chapter of Job, after passing through all of his trials and tribulations, Job could finally conclude: 'I know that

You can do all things, and that no purpose of Yours can be thwarted' *(Job 42:2)*. This is just as true today as it was for Job.

"For half my life I didn't want too much God. Now He permeates my life and all I can do is praise Him. Do you think I wanted that to happen? No! I wanted to keep all of my money! I wanted to be wealthy. I wanted to fly around in my own Lear Jet and vacation as often as I wished. That isn't asking too much, is it? But God had other plans for me. He promised to direct my path through *my entire life*. He didn't call me just to be a businessman. He used my business to direct *my life*. It is true that God gave me the personality to run a business. I didn't have any training for it. I didn't have a father that I could use as a model. It was God who gave me the personality and the DNA necessary to do what He was directing me to do—just like he has gifted you with your artistic talent.

"But God's ways are not our ways. I had absolutely no inkling that God would someday lead me to be involved with an orphanage in Myanmar (formerly known as Burma), or a home in the United States to provide support and care to young women and single mothers with children. I not only had no notion to do that, I didn't have any desire to do that. But God's ways are different from our ways. His plan is so far beyond our understanding. It was impossible for me to know fifty years ago that God would bring me into this business, and that the business would be successful, and then He would gently and progressively transform my heart, and finally work all of it to accomplish His will: not only in my life, but the lives of families and children elsewhere. ALL of that is part of His master plan, yet we only see tiny glimpses of it at any point in time, and this can only be viewed as His *current* leading for us."

I stopped. I could tell that my companion was growing fidgety over something. I quietly looked at him for a moment, and then asked:

"What is it that God is stirring you to ask?"

He looked down at his hands and remained silent for nearly a full minute. Finally, a blast of air gushed from his slight frame, as though he had been holding his breath since the meeting began.

"You keep talking about 'God's will' and 'God's good pleasure' as though everyone understands these terms. Well, THAT'S MY PROBLEM! I *don't* understand what God's will is! If I can't get clear in my head what 'God's will' means, then how can I ever expect to know if I am in His will for my life? This is what makes things so frustrating."

I said, "Fair enough. The answer to that question is simple, but the profoundly liberating consequences of the answer in your life will take a while to adjust to.

"God's **WILL** and good pleasure—lived in and through your life—is so much greater than what we will ever understand on this earth. We get a glimpse of this truth, the older we get, and have the opportunity to look back. We can see how certain life-experiences, in hindsight, were really God accomplishing something wonderful in us, but we didn't recognize it at the time. God is blessing our lives daily. Scripture tells us that He 'has blessed us with every spiritual blessing in the heavenly places in Christ' *(Ephesians 1:3)*. As we live our life, we progressively recognize His blessings manifested *in us*.

"When my business is declining, God is blessing me by growing His faith in me, and by gently and progressively working to detach me from my idolatrous dependency on my income, and in the things of this world, that I may have set up as replacements to God in my life. These are the things that fill my life with stress and unhappiness. In this sense, His working in me is synonymous with His blessing and His **WILL**.

"When my business is growing, God is blessing me by exposing my prideful lust for more. He is blessing me by miraculously working in my heart: to change my selfish desire to keep *all* the money for myself, and giving me a greater desire to help others. Again, His working in me is synonymous with His blessing and **WILL**.

"So, whether my business is growing, declining, or going out of business and I've become an employee of someone else, He is doing His good work in me. This is His good pleasure and blessing for me. What we often fail to realize is this fundamental spiritual reality: *He is ALWAYS at work in us!* Philippians 2:13 says, 'For it is God who is at work *in you*, both to **WILL** and to *work* for His *good pleasure.*' At any given moment during any given day, and throughout our entire life, God is at work in us, to **WILL** and to *work* for His *good pleasure.*

"Now, notice the similarities between Philippians 2:13 and Isaiah 46:9–10, where God Himself is speaking a promise: 'My *purpose* will be established, and I will *accomplish* all My *good pleasure.*' The words 'purpose/good pleasure' in Isaiah are synonymous with '**WILL**/good pleasure' in Philippians. His **WILL**, His purpose, and His good pleasure are all the same. Likewise, His 'work' (in Philippians) is not performed in vain—it 'accomplishes' (in Isaiah) His purpose/**Will**/good pleasure. Notice that the common phrase 'good pleasure,' in both of these verses is synonymous with God accomplishing His **Will** *and work* within us *(see also Hebrews 13:20–21).*

"In earlier years as a Christian, I completely misunderstood what the term 'God's **Will**' actually meant. I thought of God's **Will** as either: (a) *where* He wanted me to go and *what* He desired me to do, or (b) in terms of a 'perfection' that I should strive to align myself with. I never contemplated the scriptural definition in this verse: that God's **Will** *is His progressive* and continuous *working in me.* What a wonderful paradigm shift this truth created in me!

"The Freedom Truth contained in this verse is revolutionary. It means that you can *never* fall out of God's **Will** for your life. God's **Will** *lives* in you! Is it possible for your flesh to rise up and act sinfully? Yes, we all experience this every day. But can this sinful action remove you from God's **Will**? *Never!* Why is this irrevocable truth? Because God's **Will** is not dependent on our performance in living up to what we think He wants us to do (or in somehow aligning ourselves with Him). In this verse, God's **Will** is referring to *His working in us for His good pleasure.* If we find ourselves in the midst of a sinful thought or action, God IS also simultaneously active within us to **Will** and to work for His good pleasure.

"I can still vividly remember my early days of struggle, when I chased the idolatrous gods of money and success. I sought after those idols for decades until I was burned out and could go no further. I didn't know, at the time, that I was clinging to those twin idols in my heart and they were the source of my misery. But God knew. He knew that they were robbing me of true joy and peace in Him.

"Could I change any of this by myself? No. Well then, was it God's WILL that I engage in all of this degradation and sin, or be miserable, exhausted, and suffer through those many decades of hellish frustration on my own? The answer to this question is also a resounding no. But Almighty God knew, before the foundation of the world, every sin in my heart, every thorn in my flesh, every selfish decision I would make, and every idol I would chase. He knew it *all* and still chose to give me eternal life anyway.

"Let me explain this principle with a practical illustration. Let's say I have a pair of salt and pepper shakers, full to the brim with salt and pepper, respectively, and made of glass so we can see the contents. The Apostle Paul says 'that nothing good dwells in me, that is, in my flesh' *(Romans 7:18)*. This is something Christ knew about you and me before He created the foundations of the world. He knew that through Adam's fall we would inherit a sin nature—a fully depraved nature—and that we would have nothing good in us apart from Christ's life. In terms of this illustration, we would be the shaker full of pepper.

"Now, do any of the flakes in that pepper shaker surprise God? Of course, not! He knows every *single flake* of pepper in that shaker. He knew that I would lust after money, and another person would lust after alcohol, or pills, or sex. He knew that this person would verbally abuse his wife, and that person would have no patience, and that person would have three abortions, and that person would get divorced and remarried six times. He knows the lies, the deceit, the improper motives, and the hidden agendas.

He knows every flake of sin in that pepper shaker. Yet He chose us anyway—*every believer in Christ*—to be His children and vessels of His mercy.

"When God puts Christ in us to indwell us, having fully paid the price for all of those peppery flakes, God sees our little pepper shaker as though it has been freshly cleaned and already filled to the brim with the pure white salt of Christ. That is the *exchanged life* which Paul is sharing with us in 2 Corinthians 5:21. In *The Living Bible* it reads, 'For God took the sinless Christ and poured into Him our sins. Then, in exchange, He poured God's goodness into us!' This is God's perspective of our sins: They've *all* been dealt with already. He poured *all* of our peppery sins into the salt shaker representing Christ, and in exchange, poured all of Christ's pure white salt into the shaker formerly filled with pepper, but now made clean and new, representing us.

"As I say, this is God's eternal perspective of our sins, but what about sin from our experiential point of view? From our perspective, as we live our lives day to day, we still live in our human bodies, or what scripture refers to as 'earthen vessels' and the Apostle Paul calls the *flesh*. From our temporal perspective, God's placement of Christ in us is not an instantaneous 'all at once' house cleaning in terms of our capacity to act in a sinless manner. It may be easier to understand the reality if we think of it as God planting Christ *as a seed* in us. This divine seed—which contains all the fullness of Christ—is abiding completely within us yet, like a seed, is continually growing and bearing His fruit in our lives. It is God who has planted and it is God who is giving the growth. We are simply the earth that the seed is growing in. We often look at ourselves and see nothing but dirt, but God has made us precisely the way He made us to be rich soil to grow His seed of Christ in us for His glory.

"When scripture says that God is at work in us, this is what it is talking about. In the midst of all of those peppery flakes, Christ comes into my life and begins a good work in me; that is to say, He begins to grow and transform my life into His image. He bears the fruit of the Spirit within me (Galatians 5:22) in terms of love, joy, peace, patience, kindness, goodness, faithfulness, gentleness, and long-suffering. He is the faithful husbandman to care for us through sunny and rainy times, and gently, in His appointed season, bears forth His new life in place of those peppery flakes. This is something He does continuously and progressively, over the course of a person's entire life, to manifest more and more of His divine salt in our little shaker. He is the salt as a seed growing and dealing, flake by flake, with the pepper in our lives. He always works at His pace, but always continuously and progressively, to replace a grain of pepper with a grain of salt. That process won't be complete until glory, according to Romans 7, but it is His present and continuous work in us.

"This is God's WILL, according to Philippians 2:13. God's WILL is nothing less than our patient and loving God 'working for His good pleasure' in each of His children, *despite all of the flesh* and sin that might be manifest from time to time during their lives. You can't kick Him out of your life, so you can never avoid being in His WILL for you."

I wish I could report that this young artist left my office leaping and dancing and praising God. He didn't. But he left with plenty to think about.

May you begin to look at your work or business in the context of your entire life and God's faithful caring for you, and how it is impossible to disappoint Him or to stray outside His will. These three Kingdom Truths are God's formula for life-long security and happiness.

Phase II:

*Peace in our workplace flows from
peace in God's workplace.*

Chapter Five:

How Does God Define Success?

(A heart on its knees)

The wisdom from above is first pure, then peace-able, gentle, reasonable, full of mercy and good fruits, unwavering, without hypocrisy.

JAMES 3:17

There is probably no greater quixotic notion in all of human thought than the concept of "success." We've all found ourselves under its allure—perhaps in our job, or our educational endeavors, or our home life. We've all thought, *if only*: I could get that training I need (or that certificate or diploma), *then* I'll get that job I want…or *if only* I could get that raise, *then* I'd finally get ahead…or *if only* I could have more time with my family, *then* I wouldn't argue with my spouse and the kids wouldn't be rebellious…or *if only* I could be free to retire and pursue my favorite hobbies…*then* I'd be happy.

No place is the word *success* used more than in business, but what does it really mean? Surely, a quick look at a *Webster's Dictionary* will clear up everything. Let's check: the word *success* in *Webster's* means a "degree or measure of succeeding," or "one that succeeds." Hmm, don't you love it when a dictionary uses a variant of the same word they are defining as part of the definition? How about the word *successful*; maybe that will clarify things and shine light on the subject. *Webster's* tells us that *successful* means "gaining or having gained success." Well, that clears things up, doesn't it? Let's try *succeed*; we have to read deep into the definition of this word to reach its secondary meaning "to turn out well," or "attain a desired object or end" (the primary meaning relates to "following after something that has gone before," which has nothing to do with our topic).

I won't belabor this point further. I think you get the picture. Success, apart from the examples given us in scripture, is a nebulous thing. It is something that everyone believes they understand, yet few can enunciate what it *truly* means. As you read this chapter, what is your definition of success? If it is *Webster's* definition, to "attain a desired object or end," is this equally true regardless of the consequences that result? Does it remain true regardless of the moral and human cost required to achieve that end? Or would you also factor in the toll that this "achievement" takes on your marriage, your family and friends, and your personal (mental, emotional, physical and spiritual) health? After all, most people think of success and happiness as synonymous. Doesn't success equal happiness? Certainly the "success" we desire (or the goals we set) are supposed to result in the *happiness* we want and need. Success, in our thinking, is a means to an end.

In my own life, the pursuit of success and happiness once took the form of an insatiable craving for "more" of everything—*more* money, *more* expensive homes, *more* impressive hunting trophies, *more* sexual gratification, *more* respect from my wife and kids, *more* self-esteem. Yet despite all my best efforts, I *never* found what I was looking for. Possessing all of these *external* things never brought me *internal* peace or happiness. The so-called goal of success remained distant, and meaningful satisfaction eluded me. Regardless of the outcome I sought, the result left me emotionally drained, stressed-out, and continually wondering when, or if, *more* would *ever* finally be...*enough*.

Perhaps your experience is similar to mine—the more we strive for the things we assume are the indicators of success, the less peace and happiness we experience. This tells me that the common understanding of this term *success* has been inflated and distorted beyond commonsense recognition, and its use has proliferated to the point where it is often loosely associated with things that have little or nothing to do with *true success*. For the Christian business person, this is a *very serious contemplation*. For those who are not in business, the principle is the same. As we live our lives—active in whatever endeavor—are we following a "success compass" that is leading us toward *true success* or a *false illusion*? How does God define *true success* in scripture? Let's use Solomon's life from the Old Testament to gain insight into three essential attributes of *true success*:

First: *True success* is linked to God's wisdom.
In places too numerous to mention within the limited space of this book, scripture uses the term "wisdom" as closely synonymous with the concept of "success." "For wisdom is better than jewels; and all desirable things cannot compare with her *(Proverbs 8:11)*." This makes logical sense when you think about it. Can *God's wisdom* be anything other than successful? Or is there any *true success* apart from *God's wisdom*? Look at it from either direction and you reach the same conclusion: Scripture reflects a *wisdom-success* linkage that is undeniable. As we will see in more detail in a moment, probably the most successful businessman in the history of the ancient world was Solomon. And what was Solomon uniquely famous for? *His wisdom!*

Second: *True wisdom-success* is a gift from God.
The incredible wisdom-success of Solomon was not only recognized during his lifetime, but is still acknowledged today. During his life, rulers traveled from around the known world to give him gifts and listen to his counsel. What is less commonly known, however, is the fact that Solomon's wisdom wasn't entirely natural born, but was the result of him asking God for it. Wisdom was given to Solomon as a *gift from God*. In this, Solomon had no boast— for both the prompting and the giving was entirely sourced from God. Solomon's wisdom was really God's wisdom given to him as a gift.

If you read of Solomon's life in the books of Kings and Chronicles, you will soon discover a great example of the *wisdom-success* connection I am talking about: "Now, Solomon loved the Lord, walking in the statutes of his father David [which means he had a loving heart for God's word just as his father King David did]" *(1 Kings 3:3)*. One night, following the death of his father, God appeared to Solomon in a dream and prompted him to "Ask what you wish me to give you" *(1 Kings 3:5)*.

Solomon was a very young man at the time, about twenty years old, when his father died and he became king of Israel. Had God asked me that question in my twenties I would have asked for immense wealth and fortune, or great fame and honor, or an invincible army, or retribution and revenge against those I didn't like, or if He caught me on a day when my allergies were acting up, I might have asked for a long and healthy life. Come to think of it, since God didn't limit the request to only one thing, I probably would have asked for all of it at once. But scripture tells us that Solomon asked for none of those things. In response to God's prompting, he only asked for a solitary gift from God: *He asked for wisdom (1 Kings 3:6–9)*. And this was not for himself, but for the purpose of better serving God's people. You can read the full narrative in First Kings; God not only gave Solomon the wisdom he asked for in abundance, but also gave him things that he didn't ask for, such as riches and honor, if he would "walk in My ways, keeping My statues and commandments, as your father David walked, then I will prolong your days" *(1 Kings 3:10–14)*. God knew that *His wisdom* and *true success* are intrinsically linked.

Third: *True wisdom-success* is progressively revealed by God.

The third attribute of *true success* from Solomon's life is that the wisdom God gave to Solomon was not an all-inclusive, one-time historical event, but rather a "just-in-time" *progressive* revelation of God's wisdom in Solomon's life. We have already read about God's initial grant of wisdom to Solomon in 1 Kings 3:10-14, but then in chapter five, when Solomon was dealing with Hiram King of Tyre, we read: "The Lord gave [present tense] wisdom to Solomon, just as He promised him; and there was peace between Hiram and Solomon, and the two of them made a covenant" (1 Kings 5:12). When Solomon had need of wisdom to negotiate a peace agreement with the King of Tyre, God gave him the wisdom he needed when he needed it for each different situation he faced.

God also brought wisdom to Solomon through the agency of others. In 1 Kings 7:14 we read of a man named Hiram (not to be confused with Hiram the King of Tyre): "He was a widow's son from the tribe of Naphtali, and his father was a man of Tyre, a worker in bronze; and he was *filled with wisdom and understanding and skill* for doing any work in bronze. So he came to King Solomon and performed all his work." When Solomon had need of specific wisdom, in the form of unique skills or understanding, God provided the wisdom he needed by delivering the right person to Solomon at the right time. Again, God was faithful to progressively provide wisdom when, where, and in the form that Solomon needed at the time.

True *wisdom-success* results when God directs your path. We see from scripture concerning Solomon's life that when God orders your life, you are successful. As God establishes, guides, and directs your footsteps in His word *(Psalm 119:133)*, you experience the *wisdom-success* that only

God can give you; and your life naturally bears the fruit of this *wisdom-success*. I love the wonderful metaphor in Psalm 1:3, of the man who meditates on God's word day and night. Read this verse and consider how accurately it describes King David, Solomon, *and us*: "He will be like a tree *firmly* planted by streams of water, which *yields its fruit* in its season and its leaf does not wither; and in whatever he does, *he prospers*." Jeremiah 17:7–8 echoes this metaphor: "Blessed is the man who trusts in the Lord and whose trust *is* the Lord. For he will be like a tree planted by the water, that extends its roots by a stream and will not fear when the heat comes; but its leaves will be green, and it will not be anxious in a year of drought *nor cease to yield fruit*."

As God's people of faith, these verses also *describe us*, whose life is full of God's word and His trust within us concerning His progressive directing of our lives. We are not described as gazelles running about, but as a tree *firmly* planted. We are not likened to a tumble weed tossed to-and-fro by dry winds in a desert land, but of a strong and healthy tree, planted by God near His source of living water, with deep roots, and vibrant green leaves, and un-failing fruit—all of which is a beautiful picture of a *fully prosperous life*—a life that bears the fruits of God in it: God's peace, God's joy, and God's fulfillment, to name but a few.

God's *wisdom-success* is available to us today—and every day!

Are you thinking that such a prosperous life was given only to Solomon? Think again. Solomon's life was only a precur-sor of *our lives*—a glimpse of what every true Christian's life is today. The divine wisdom that Solomon received as a gift from God was but a tiny fraction of the wisdom God has given to us. In 1 Corinthians 1:30 we read: "But by His doing you are in Christ Jesus, who became to us *wisdom from God*...." God has now placed every believer into Christ Jesus, who possesses all of the omniscient wisdom of God. This means that wisdom-success for the Christian is *not* a thing or an achievement, *but a person*. It is Christ living His wisdom filled life out in our lives—wisely guiding and directing our paths through every situation, circumstance, and challenge we face on a daily basis.

Wisdom is, in the vernacular of the day, what God would do in every situation—it is *daily and situational guidance* from God. A few years ago, there was sort of a fad going around in the local churches. You saw it on bumper stickers and on the internet: "WWJD?" was the phrase. The first time I saw this acronym I thought it was a radio station, but I soon realized that it stood for the question: What Would Jesus Do? Now, I acknowledge from a theological perspective that there are those who would say that this is entirely the *wrong* question to ask, and I am not suggesting that you start asking yourself this question. But I do think it is a good starting point when thinking about what wisdom is in practical terms. *Wisdom from God, in its simplest terms, is what God would do if He were in my shoes.* Would God make this decision? If so, how would He make it? How would God speak to this or that issue? Or would He speak to it at all? As we will see in the rest of this chapter, the fact is: God is not separate and distant from us; He is present *in us*. He *is* walking in your shoes, just as He *is* walking in mine.

If God has called me to business, then that means He has called me to deal with the material things of business: sales, cash flow, financial planning, government regulations, re-cruiting, hiring, customer service, public relations, problem solving, and the daunting task of trying to grow a business, if possible, in recessionary times. When 1 Corinthians 1:30 tells us that God has given us *wisdom from God*, then that wisdom is intended for our use right now, and includes what God would do in all of these circumstances, not only in business, but for every aspect of our lives. This awesome, omniscient wisdom resides in each of us and never leaves us. The Spirit of the Living God dwells within us *(Romans 8:9)*, and is faithfully working this wisdom-success into our lives. We can rest in the fact that God is constantly at work in us to will and to work for His good pleasure *(Philippians 2:13)*, which means He is continously working His wisdom-success within us. We don't have to figure it out, or strain to know it, or strive more to achieve it. The bottom line is this: *God defines success as the practical and progressive application of His wisdom—as daily and situational guidance—to our lives.*

Does this sound impossible or impractical to you?

You may be saying, "Okay, great. I need wisdom. So, how do I get this wisdom? How do I get in touch with it? How do I become intuitive enough, or introspective enough, or whatever I need to do, to be able to read it or listen to it within me? It's fine to say that Christ is God's wisdom and He lives in me; I see that in scripture and I'm grateful for it. But how do I tap into this so-called *daily and situational guidance from God* in practical terms? God hasn't spoken to me out of a burning bush lately. When you are talking about wisdom, you are talking about a divine attribute of God, which I hope to experience more in glory, but my experience tells me that it's not something available down in the nitty-gritty life that I'm living now. This may work for you, Daryl, but it's too mystical for me. When I'm in the middle of a heated crisis at work or at home, I need something practical, not a theory that's impossible to access or understand in real time. No offense, but this sounds a bit like spiritual mumbo-jumbo to me."

Right now, as I am writing this, I have a big smile on my face. I can't tell you how many times I've heard some variation of this response, and it reflects exactly where my thinking was for the first thirty years of my Christian life. But think about it. Does it make any logical sense, even in human terms? For this response to be true: God would have gone through all of the trouble to send His Son to die for us, adopt us as children in His household *(Ephesians 1:5)*, then place us in Christ and give Christ to us as our *wisdom from God*, then send the Holy Spirit to us as our Comforter, Helper, and Guide *(John 14:26, 15:26; Romans 5:5, 8:26-27; Ephesians 1:13)*—and then after accomplishing all of this—proceed to hide this very same wisdom from His own children so we can't access it for anything practical until after we are dead, buried, and in glory? For those of you who are parents, is that what you would do to your own children—make them wait until they are dead and buried before you are willing to help them?

I can share with you today some glorious good news from scripture. Wisdom from our Heavenly Father is not mystical, hidden, or complicated. It's practical and down-to-earth. I readily acknowledge that it took decades for the light to finally "come on" in my own head about this. But God progressively brought me to the realization that the *wisdom of God*—who created everything, knows everything, sees everything, and has the loving desire for me to experience true love, joy, peace, gentleness, kindness, and *true success*—has put *within me* everything necessary to experience this fullness *right now*. He hasn't hidden it out there in the universe somewhere separate and apart from me. He hasn't delayed the enjoyment of its benefits until glory. I know how easy it is to think of God's wisdom only as something outside of us—as being *external* and not *internal* to us—but that is simply not scriptural. It's not the whole truth. God's wisdom *is also available within us* as a practical benefit for our daily living.

When this reality first dawned on me, it simply blew my mind. I was awestruck, to realize that all of the wisdom of God—what He would do in every situation and every circumstance, and all of the knowledge to do everything right (that is, righteous)—dwells in me, and is available to me for guiding my daily living. How to deal with my kids abides in me. How to face every negative situation resides in me. All of those practical decisions I need to make on a daily basis—are in me. It blows my mind just thinking about it.

For the remainder of this chapter let's explore more specifically how God works His wisdom-success into our lives; and how He draws us into a deeper understanding of how to access it on a daily basis.

Why don't we hear God's wisdom all the time?

This is best explained, in part, by the use of an analogous example. Have you ever been sitting in a public gathering of people, let's say in a movie theater, or a large lecture hall at school, or a church auditorium, and the film is playing or the teacher/pastor is speaking in the front of the room and you are trying to listen attentively. But the people in the row directly behind you are whispering, sniggering, and generally paying no attention to the movie/lecture/message at all. They seem content to take interminable turns reaching deep into their crinkly bags of candy for yet another sweet. Whoever is immediately behind you is unquestionably in the thralls of an active cold or flu. You can feel the breeze from his relentless (and uncovered) hacking cough on the back of your neck. Every so often, the one behind you to your left begins to cry, sometimes in a whimper and other times in dramatic sobs, and decides that you are her best source for an urgent supply of tissues. The one behind you on your right is the intellectual of the group (if only she would listen). She taps you on the shoulder from time to time to ask for clarification of what was just said from the front of the room, or to whisper some critical comment she finds important. Every time you turn sidewise to give them a tissue, or listen to a comment or question, your focus slips. By the time you turn back to refocus on the movie or speaker, you've missed a portion of the story/message being shared. The people in back of you aren't preventing the movie from being played, or the teacher/pastor from delivering his or her message, but they are making it frustratingly difficult for you to remain focused and personally hear and understand in a way that would be optimally beneficial to you.

I think this is a good example of the relentless antics we all experience from our flesh, and how these antics serve to disrupt our focus on, and understanding of, God's wisdom. God's wisdom is always there and He is continually sharing this wisdom with us, but our flesh is so self-absorbed and noisome within its own frenetic activity *apart from God* that it often obfuscates the message and frustrates our ability to recognize God's speaking in practical terms. Can our flesh ultimately succeed in preventing God from doing His good pleasure in us? No way! We are talking about Almighty God here. Greater is He who is in us than he who is in the world *(1 John 4:4)*. Even at times when the flesh seems hyperactive, with all of its worry and fretting, it can never prevail over the Spirit of the How-Great-Thou-Art God in our spirit. We don't have to "help" the Holy Spirit prevail; we don't have to work at it ourselves as though the Holy Spirit is impotent, or try to figure out a strategy for dealing with our flesh by using our human logic. God is certainly able to deal with the antics of our flesh on His own.

What has been helpful in my experience, however, is being brought into a clearer understanding by God: how He goes about quieting the flesh and making His wisdom known to us. As we get a clearer picture of the former, it greatly expands our sensitivity to the latter. To understand God's work in this regard, it is first helpful to understand what scripture refers to as our "flesh" and how this flesh goes about distracting us from God's guiding wisdom.

What is our flesh?
I warn you in advance that this is not a pleasant topic. You may experience an overpowering desire to put this book down at numerous places over the next few pages. The flesh always gets uncomfortable when it is exposed to the light of scripture. But think of this next section as a mephitic smelling slumgullion of vitamins, minerals, and

phytonutrients that your medical doctor has prescribed to strengthen your immune system: it won't take long to read, but it is enormously helpful for anyone led by God to seek greater understanding about the *operation of true wisdom-success in their lives.*

Our flesh is the "collection" of all our *human* wisdom, talent, physical energy, habits, desires, emotional feelings, psychologies, thought processes, and volitional inclinations, which we rely upon *apart from God.*

This collection is everything that represents *who we are* apart from God's saving work in us. I think we would all agree that while this collection may be combined differently in each of us—that is to say, we all possess varying degrees of both positive and negative personal attributes—the overall collection is essentially the same. One person's "flesh" is basically the same as the next person's flesh. The senior pastor's flesh is the same as the new believer's flesh, and it remains the flesh throughout their lives. My flesh is the same now as it was when I was twenty. It attempts to entice me in different ways, but it is still the same old flesh.

Sorry to say, the pitfalls of the flesh are legion: *pride* (needing to be "right"); *fear* (needing to maintain the respect of others); *impatience* (needing to make this or that decision *right now*); and *selfish ambition* (any motive, thought, or desire within us that wants to gain a personal advantage or benefit). Add to these things other emotional attributes like *anger...resentment...jealousy...worry,* and the list goes on. You begin to get the picture of how pervasive and insidious the flesh really is.

We may command extraordinary talents and intelligence. We may possess impressive personal qualities, unbounded energy, and positive mental attitudes. But we likely also possess within our heart a deeper collection of ugly things as well. For some, it may be pride that dominates. For others it may be greed, selfishness, or anger that leads the way. Still others may be naturally inclined to criticize the imperfections of others, rather than acknowledge with humility their own flaws. They may cry for justice, and prefer to pursue revenge rather than forgiveness, when suffering a perceived wrong. All of this, part positive and part negative (and in whatever combination) is what scripture refers to as "the flesh." From God's perspective, all of this is sourced from unrighteous *impurities* emanating *from the heart.*

While these *impurities* can often appear disguised to the point where we scarcely perceive their presence, or perhaps we interpret them as "appropriate" or "acceptable" under the circumstances, nevertheless they are responsible for generating *one-hundred percent* of the stress we experience in our daily lives. *That's right...100% of the stress in our lives comes from this source.* Such things as leadership stress, marital stress, parenting stress, coworker stress, and self-esteem stress are just a few of the stresses that flow from this fleshly fount. These impurities rob us of peace and joy; they disrupt our relationships with others, and heap unbearable burdens on every aspect of our personal and professional lives.

For example, take the granddaddy of them all in my own life: *pride.*

Like every expression of the flesh, pride concerns itself with what makes *us* feel good; it whispers its earthly "wisdom" into our thoughts based on how a situation will

ultimately benefit us personally. This may include our professional goals, or certain personal priorities, such as how
much time we spend pursuing hobbies, recreation, sports,
physical workouts, shopping, church work ... even devotional time. Pride says, "I need to *do* this," or, "I need to
have this," without giving due regard to the needs of other
people or to the promptings of the Holy Spirit within us. It
leads us to see others, not as individual *people* whom God
has created and loves, but as *objects* which are either *helping*
us accomplish what *we* want or *preventing* us from doing
so. Of course, pride conceals itself in all manner of nuance,
pleasantries, and the appearance of unassailable good intentions; but at its core, we find nothing more than fleshly
self-absorption.

Pride convinces us, "Life is what *I* make of it"; "God
helps those who help *themselves*"; "It's *my* responsibility to
take care of *Number One*." It leads us to observe others in
a judgmental light, and to exaggerate (or inwardly boast
about) our own good qualities by comparison. Pride wants
what it wants *now,* and is jealous when others have something that we don't have. Pride relentlessly lobbies for the
newest, biggest, fanciest, and most expensive. It selectively
filters what we hear from others, and the words we choose
to speak in response (and yes, even the tone we choose to
speak them in). It influences the way we make decisions,
both in terms of the actions we take and those we don't.

And from a spiritual point of view, because pride is
completely self-absorbed—*if it could*—it would inhibit us
from truly trusting God in *every* situation that we find ourselves. I use the term "if it could" on purpose, of course,
because by God's mercy our fleshly and willful pride is

never stronger than God's will for us. He is always working to grow His trust in us. Like the Israelite's journey through the wilderness and into the Promised Land, God is working every circumstance in our lives to increase our trust and peace in Him as we travel on His ever-brightening path that leads deeper into Him *(Proverbs 4:18).*

From our human wisdom, to the extent that we admit to pride at all, we consider it a relative term to what we see displayed in others. By this comparison, we "wisely" conclude, as we observe someone else, that we surely are not *that proud;* so, we must be living a pretty decent Christian life overall. We may not be perfect inwardly, but no one sees that part of us anyway. We definitely are much closer to being *functionally* perfect outwardly than most other Christians we know. Certainly, that is good enough to maintain our Christian testimony, isn't it? All of this kind of logic is broadly viewed in scripture as our human or *earthly wisdom.*

Earthly wisdom.
Here is what James has to say about the nature of our human, earthly wisdom:

> If you have bitter jealousy and selfish ambition *in your heart*, do not be arrogant and so lie against the truth. *This wisdom* **is not that which comes down from above, but is** *earthly, natural, demonic.* For where jealousy and selfish ambition exist, *there is disorder and every evil thing.*
>
> JAMES 3:14–16

Remember that "God is not a God of confusion but of peace" *(1 Corinthians 14:33)*. James highlights a sobering truth here: that *any* impulse of the flesh, *any* lack of purity that remains operational in our hearts, inevitably manifests the fruit of *disorder and every evil thing*. Wow! Our inner thoughts and attitudes are far more important to peace-filled living than we thought. In fact, such things produce *disorder* in our lives and that *disorder* affects the lives of those around us. We don't live in a vacuum. Any anger we harbor, for example, creates defensiveness and emotional distance in others; self-ishness often breeds distrust; and so on.

When we foster anger toward our spouses for not meeting some perceived need, or lash out at the kids for coming home late, we distance ourselves from the very people that we say we love the most. We may feel justified in acting the way we do, but we are nevertheless undermining the mutual love and respect inherent in the supportive communication so critical to family life. We are introducing *disorder and every evil thing* into our own family, such as feelings of failure and inadequacy, suspicion, doubt, guilt, anger, and resentment, none of which is easily or quickly overcome.

Wisdom from above.
God's mercy in James 3:17 describes a truly good-news alternative for us:

> The *wisdom* from above is *first* pure, then peaceable, gentle, reasonable, full of mercy and good fruits, unwavering, without hypocrisy.

In this verse, James describes God's radically different approach to life: one rooted, not in the flesh, but in a continuous, heartfelt, experiential knowledge of God. It is an approach that bears God's fruit—all of the fruit mentioned in this verse and more—in our lives. As we have already seen from 1 Corinthians 1:30, this *wisdom* as James calls it, is *nothing less than Christ's own life,* manifest *in and through us.*

Now, I used to think that the primary evidence for whether I was living a successful Christian life was the Bible studies I held at work, the Sunday school classes I taught at church, the neighbors I witnessed to from time to time, and the fact that I drove around in my fancy new *Cadillac* with a fish sticker on the bumper. But as God opened my eyes to these verses in James and in 1 Corinthians, I began to see what a *true* life in Christ is all about.

Successful Christian living doesn't flow from *my* ambitious human efforts for God (that is, *from* what is "earthly, natural, and demonic" as described in James 3), but *from above.* Wisdom from above is sourced from where? From us? No, we are earthly and natural. This wisdom comes from where James says it comes from: *from above.* And it is first and foremost: *pure.* Note that scripture doesn't say that the wisdom that comes from above is first "balanced," as though the key to successful Christian living is bringing all of life's disparate activities, including a cubicle for God, into balance with one another. *Pure wisdom from above is certainly the source of balance in our lives,* although we will likely not be aware of it in those terms, *but balance is never the source of purity or wisdom.* Wisdom that comes down from God is, in its *first* instance, a matter of *purity* of heart.

Putting to death the deeds of the flesh.

By comparing James 3:14–16 with James 3:17, we recognize that James is setting up a comparison between two sources of wisdom. One source is earthly, natural, and demonic *(James 3:15)* and bears the fruit of disorder and every evil thing. The other is from above *(James 3:17)*, and bears all manner of Godly fruit. The crucible containing these two warring paradigms of "wisdom" is our heart (James 3:14). The "purity" James is talking about relates to the *absence of* impure earthly wisdom, which we have already considered under the synonym of the *flesh*.

A pure heart is one that desires, more than anything else, to simply *know* God and experience *His* life. And because every manifestation of our flesh (no matter how seemingly insignificant) interferes with that life, a pure heart means, by extension, that the Holy Spirit is putting to death any earthly "life" that is sourced from our own flesh.

> If you are living according to the flesh, you must die; but if *by the Spirit* you are putting to death the deeds of the body, *you will live.*
> Romans 8:13

Thank God, the good news of this verse is that the Spirit of God, not us, is the power that puts to death the deeds of the flesh. That includes death to every agenda of our own, and every effort to justify ourselves or to "look good" in the eyes of others. It includes our thinking that the situation we find ourselves in has somehow evaded God's control, and therefore, requires our intervention to "fix it" so life can run smoothly again. It includes every thought that life would be easier if that *other* person would only do something different, or pay more attention to how their actions affect us, or that someone or something (other than us) is to blame for the way we happen to be thinking, feeling, or acting at the moment. All of these antics of the flesh oppose God's life in us because they draw our attention off of Christ as our wisdom-success, and turn our focus to what we currently desire or think we need. To put this in simple terms: the enemy, or inhibitor, to experiencing *true success* in our lives *is our flesh,* and this flesh is in the process of being put to death by the Holy Spirit.

Pure wisdom, by comparison, is the Spirit of God leading us to embrace the truth, the whole truth, and nothing but the truth behind every situation. Pure wisdom draws us to perceive *everyone* as a creation of God and *everything* as God perceives it, rather than as our flesh "wants" or "needs" to perceive it. And finally, *pure wisdom* supplies the grace to respond to criticism, problems, circumstances, and challenges, including the "needs" and "flesh" of others, solely in the way that the Holy Spirit in us is prompting us to respond. It is, as Romans 8:13 puts it: *to live by the Spirit.*

What's left when the flesh is silenced in death?

Why do our thoughts often spontaneously turn to God? Why does a particular Bible verse come to mind unbidden and uninvited? Why do we pray for the things we pray for, or pray as much as we do? Or why do we cross paths with someone who says just the thing we need to hear at that moment? In my experience, it's because the Holy Spirit is in relentless combat with the flesh. He is active in seeking out and killing the deeds of our flesh, which is likewise also active in making us fearful, impatient, worried, angry, prideful, resentful, or desperate to win every argument. Every prompting by the Holy Spirit to pray, for example, is a death blow to some aspect of our flesh. Every thought of God impales a part of our flesh on the petard of faith. Every scripture verse brought to our memory contains within it the very divine power needed to bring what the verse says into being in our lives and to silence our flesh.

Now here is the truly exciting part. Have you ever considered what's left at the point when some aspect of the flesh is silenced in death? I'll give you a hint. Remember my example of sitting in that movie theater, large lecture hall, or church auditorium trying to watch a movie or listen to a speaker, while all along the people behind you would not stop their incessant blathering? What happens when the usher asks those people to leave and the row behind you becomes silent? Without you doing a thing, you can now watch the movie or hear the speaker clearly.

What is left when the flesh is silenced? All that is left is the *wisdom from above*. This really blows my mind just to think about it! The wisdom of God is automatically manifest in our lives when some aspect of our flesh is silenced in death. The Holy Spirit causes this to happen in our lives scores, if not hundreds of times every day, oftentimes without our being aware of it. That's what I never realized before. I always thought that God's wisdom was something outside of me, something I had to search for, something I had to figure out. This was always a miserable struggle, of course, because I thought God expected me to be the responsible one: to decrypt and decipher what God was trying to tell me in any particular situation.

To be honest, for decades I was convinced that I could never really know God's direction for my life clearly enough or at all. It never occurred to me that what scripture tells us is exactly the opposite! Scripture tells us that we don't have to worry about it at all. God is working tirelessly to bring His will clearly into our lives. There are only two sources of wisdom in this world: one earthly and one heavenly. What happens at the moment that the earthly wisdom from my flesh is silenced (and without me raising so much as a finger)? All that remains is the wisdom of God coming through me clear as a clarion call. I have nothing to boast—it is the *wisdom-success from above*—it is a gift from God and entirely His doing. I praise the Lord for this.

Wisdom from above leads us to walk into our next staff meeting *sensitive to the Holy Spirit*; or going to that planning meeting *sensitive to the Holy Spirit*; or handling that next telephone call *sensitive to the Holy Spirit's leading. Wisdom from above* is reviewing my financial statements, not just based on my educational training, but by being *sensitive to the Holy Spirit's leading* regarding not just the financial statements themselves, but everything else related to my life (both business and personal), because He is vastly wiser than anything on earth. Success is *living by the Spirit* as He puts to death the deeds of our flesh. This is the path God has put us on. It is a progressive path where He is renewing our minds *(Ephesians 4:23)*, and transforming us from glory to glory, even as from the Lord, the Spirit *(2 Corinthians 3:18)*.

Praying without ceasing.
As I continue through life with all of its challenges and difficulties, God has brought me more and more to a simple

place before Him. He has caused me, trained me, to be increasingly sensitive throughout my day to His divine Spirit within me. *Lord, what would you have me do concerning this matter? Are You prompting me to be quiet or to say something? Are You giving me peace about that business decision to build an office building rather than continue to lease? Lord, are You bringing up this sensitive topic in the staff meeting, or not?*

The most important thing we are called by God to do on a daily basis, whether we are in business or not, is to *simply talk to Him throughout our day, about our day.* You don't have to stop what you're doing, close your eyes, and pray out loud. You can speak to Him silently in your heart regardless of what you are doing at the time. He knows all about it before we even get out of bed in the morning, and before we get to work. As we are walking through the office and throughout the day, just by talking to the Lord about the things we are involved in is incredibly powerful in changing our hearts from our fleshly motives to Christ's pure one. For me, this is what scripture refers to as going through our day *praying without ceasing (1 Timothy 5:17).*

As I am on my way to a business meeting, I speak silently to Him, *Lord I just want your heart and your truth to be manifest in my life during this meeting.* And as your eyes turn to Him, He will make you aware that your heart holds the taint of an arrogant or judgmental spirit, or the intention to prove a point, or needing to be right, or worries about the outcome and the loss of revenue or reputation. Often, it is at that point (as the Spirit of the Lord shines His light on my heart) that I pray, "Lord, please renew a right spirit in me again."

I can't renew my own spirit, only Christ can do that by manifesting His life in me. According to James, only that which comes down from God *is pure*. The simple concept of talking to the Lord throughout the day—about our day—is something God prompts us to do. He draws us to trust Him, to speak to Him, and to listen to His speaking in our heart. It is something we can do regardless of how miserable we see ourselves spiritually at the time. Without that, we will busy ourselves in conducting meetings, replying to customers in person or over the phone, and talking to employees—but most of it will be sourced from the flesh. Yet, as the Lord develops within us this life of speaking to Him throughout the day, He leads us deeper into the abiding peace of His *true wisdom-success*. Notice that the wisdom from above is *first* pure, then *peaceable*. Experiencing calm and peace within is a hallmark of God's wisdom.

Let's put this into the context of a practical business scenario. Let's say that you come to work one morning to a heated voicemail from your largest customer. It sounds like she is a gnat's eyelash away from firing you and discontinuing your company's services. Not only is this account a significant revenue source for your business, but this particular customer is a *center of influence* within your community and may affect the decisions of some of your other customers—all because a couple of your employees have gotten increasingly sloppy with their work over the last month, which also hasn't been picked up by any of their supervisors. Your gut begins to churn acid and your mind races into an internal conversation with this customer that imagines who you will blame, and what excuses you can make, and what you will promise to salvage this account.

What's important to recognize in this scenario is that all of these tendencies are early warning signs that we are *losing our peace.* Our eyes are coming off Christ and our flesh is coming online. In reality, "success" is not about keeping this customer (or losing her), it's about the work God does in our hearts while walking through the circumstance with Him. Success is peace, rest, and relationship with God despite the outward appearance of the situation. In some cases, you keep the customer and in others you don't, but that's not God's definition of success. That's why, when such situations arise, it is a great time to return the gaze of our hearts back to Christ, and away from the person(s) we believe responsible, or whatever eventuality we fear. It is a great time to immediately ask the Lord to expose the true source of our current distress—the ongoing impurity in *our own* hearts.

How then—in a practical sense—do we do that? For me, the answer to that question lies in the prayer of the Psalmist:

> **Search me, O God**, and know my heart;
> Try me and know my anxious thoughts;
> **And see if there be any hurtful way in me,**
> *And lead me in the everlasting way.*
> PSALM 139:23-24

These precious words have become a lifeline for my soul; I find myself praying them often. Every time, they cause me to turn inward, to kneel in my heart. They expose whatever movement of my flesh is operational at that particular moment and allow Christ to manifest His superior power—His life—in its place.

Let's say, for example, that I start to have a critical thought toward someone in the office because I see them using an extended amount of company time for a personal project. Right away, my mind starts to race with negative thoughts, and my heart floods with disgust and pride; in a matter of a few moments, I'm wallowing in resentment. *Why does that person think they can do that during work hours? Don't they know they're on the payroll? After all…*

I've lost all sense of peace within, and my heart and mind are in turmoil.

This is how the Lord often guides me in the way He would have me go. He uses that loss of peace and the abrupt sense of inner turmoil as sort of a gyroscope to give balance to my thinking. He will bring to mind a verse, perhaps the Psalmist's words: "Search *me*, O God…." The divine power in that verse comes alive within me and God reveals the true nature of my resentment, which may be sourced from my own pride in the situation. I then begin to hate the way I feel. I hate that feeling of pride within me, and my corrosive hostility toward that person. By the time I get back to my desk, I am praying: Lord, *I don't want to feel this way. If there's an issue here you want me to address with that person, you'll make me know it at the appointed time. But for right now, please replace my resentment with your pure heart. Fill me with Yourself. I don't want my ugly flesh to live any longer. I only want You to be manifest in me.*

Today, the words in that Psalm are my total freedom, because the power contained within them causes me to live in a different place. I don't mean I "try" to live there, or try to "change" anything about myself. Those words are one of my continual connections with the God that I now recognize and experience as truly sovereign over every area of my life. The same could be said for scores of other verses that the Lord might bring to mind during daily circumstances. As I simply talk to Him, He is faithful to lead me in the way He would have me go *(Psalm 25:12–14)*.

A final conversation.
I am hesitant to share one final conversation with you because I don't want you to misunderstand it as my effort to boast. Still, I am going to share it because I trust the Lord to give you encouragement and hope through it. What I am about to share with you has *nothing* to do with me, and *everything* to do with God. My simple testimony to you is that if God can do this in my life, He can do it in your life. I've already shared with you how filled my life was with unquenchable lust for more and more of everything. Nothing was *ever* enough.

About five years ago, one of my vice-presidents came to my office. He had been running some numbers on several scenarios and wanted to share his findings with me. After laying before me his spreadsheets, he excitedly informed me that if I would just increase the hours I committed to work on the business by three or four hours per day—in three years, I could double, triple, or even quadruple my personal income and that of the business. A quick glance at his numbers while he was talking convinced me that he was probably right.

But I was genuinely puzzled and said, "Why would I want to do that?"

He answered with his own question, "Why wouldn't you want to do that?"

I answered, "Because I'm content" (meaning that I'm content with the way God is ordering my life).

He paused for nearly half a minute, looking straight at me, then he said simply, "Then, Daryl, you are truly the most successful person I know," and he left my office.

I consider this to be an absolute miracle of God in my life. I simply do not have the words to describe to you the depth of depravity I was consumed with regarding my lust for making money. It was destroying my marriage, my family, my health, yet I had *no power* to do anything about it. All I knew to do was saturate my system with Valium in hopes of somehow surviving the urgent stress and anxiety from the day. Literally, life was slipping through my fingers and I had no power to stop it.

Believe me, I'm not proud of this story, and I certainly don't need to embellish or dramatize it in any way—it's ugly enough as it is. There was no possible way within me to curb my lust for more. I worshipped this idol with my whole life. That is why, to this day, I can't contain my praise to God. Only He had the power to save me from my fleshly self. He has gently and progressively isolated and killed that fleshly lust in me to the point where I could honestly respond to this vice-president in the manner I did, and believe what I was saying in my heart. I have only God to praise and worship for this *wisdom from above* and its life-saving transformation on my life.

I started this chapter with how nebulous and elusive our definition of success is. After fifty years of business experience, I can tell you that God's definition of success is something very different from our own. Success for God is the progressive death of our flesh and the growth of His life in our spirit. Not His power to help us achieve our earthly goals, but His power to transform us into the image of His Son and deepen our *relational experience* with Him.

Today, a pure heart is the only place I want to live. It's the sum total of the Christian life: It is a place where I desire to decrease and for Him to increase *(John 3:30)*. It's where the freedom is. It's how scripture defines success:

Christ is everything.
Not just *more*.
But *everything*.
Our *entire* joy.
Our *entire* peace.
Our *entire* wisdom-success each day.
Where—enough is *truly* enough!

Chapter Six:

What Great Things the Lord has Done!

(God has done it all, He is all we need)

> *He said to him, "Go home to your people and*
> *report to them what great things the Lord has done*
> *for you, and how He had mercy on you."*
>
> MARK 5:19

The title of this book is *A Simplified Life* for a reason. It's not a book of exegesis, apologetics, systematic theology, or hermeneutics. It's not about any of these scholarly pursuits. All of these things, of course, are fine in their place, but that's not the focus here. This book is simply a personal testimony of *what great things the Lord has done* for one guy who has been in the care of God—most often without his knowing it and frequently in spite of himself— for over seventy years now and fifty years in business. It's not a "self-help" book because you neither need *my* help, nor are you helped by the delusion that *you* can (or need to) help yourself.

Neither is true.

The reality is much better, and is as steadfast, unchanging, and absolute as God Himself. The divine truth is: **God has done it all**, and in every circumstance and in whatever situation, **He is all we need**. Ask yourself: Do I agree with this ten-word statement, or not?

My experience has taught me that no amount of elegant words, either verbal or written, can convince another person of anything that they don't want to hear (or are not ready to hear), unless it is God's timing that they hear it. For this reason, I have no desire (even to try) to convince anyone of the truths contained in these pages. I leave the care and instruction of each reader to the loving sovereignty of the Holy Spirit and the power in God's word. This is the *only* way that any of us come to a deeper understanding of God's truth.

However, since we are in Phase II of this book, which focuses on the concept that *peace in our workplace flows from peace in God's workplace*, it may prove useful to some readers for me to highlight a number of the specific stumbling blocks that I have experienced as God led me to a greater understanding of this wonderful truth from scripture. And while I'm at it, I want to answer a few of the questions I hear most often.

I have often touched upon some variation or other of this wonderful theme, *God has done it all, He is all we need*, because I have no other explanation for my success as a businessman. I have no ten-point outline of earthly wisdom to help you on your way. As I shared in chapter one, had God left me to my earthly wisdom in running a business, I would have been dead years ago. I truly believe the stress I was creating for myself would have killed me.

Let's begin with how God has changed my approach to reading scripture. Thirty years ago, I would have read about King David declaring to God, "You have been my God from my mother's womb" *(Psalm 22:10)*; or that Christ has *already* paid the price for our sins *once and for all* through His death on the cross so He might bring us to God *(1 Peter 2:24, 3:18)*; or that God has already *forgiven and forgotten* them *(Jeremiah 31:34; Hebrews 8:12, 10:17)*; or that He has separated us from those transgressions as far as the East is from the West *(Psalm 103:12)*; and that there is now *no condemnation* for those who are in Christ Jesus *(Romans 8:1)*. I would have read these verses and mentally discounted them as directed to someone else or to a future time (but not now).

When I read these verses today, I see wonderfully liberating verses regarding what God has accomplished on our behalf and His loving care for us. Yet for the first several decades of my early Christian life, I didn't recognize the liberating power in those verses at all. I still felt guilty and condemned by the sins I inevitably committed each day. Doesn't Romans 8:1 make an unambiguous statement that *there is now **no condemnation** for those who are in Christ Jesus*? Yes, it does say that, and the verse is absolute and unconditional. But I operated under a set of *presuppositions* that governed my perception of the world around me, including the scriptural verses I read.

Presuppositions rob us of liberty in Christ.
A *presupposition* occurs when we *take for granted* (or assume) that certain things are true *before* we actually know what

the facts are. These preliminary assumptions—whether they are true or not doesn't matter—skew any subsequent understandings we might derive from the facts that follow. They create a *selective perception* within us that *filters* all future information we receive. For example, when we see a car stopped on the side of the road with a police car behind it with flashing lights, we assume that this driver has been pulled over for speeding or some other traffic violation. In fact, the car may only have a flat tire and the officer is assisting the motorist by slowing the traffic to make the area safer while the motorist (or the officer) changes the tire. Our initial *presupposition* about the entire scene was false.

When reading scripture, we can do the same thing. We are tempted to *presuppose* what a verse means, rather than read it with an open heart and mind for what it actually says; and ask God to imprint on our hearts His faith to believe what the verse truly declares.

I'll use my own testimony here, as an example, to make this concept easier to understand. Prior to my salvation experience, I didn't give much thought to the concept of "sin" on a personal level. Of course, my dad was an evangelical preacher so I heard the term many times, but in my perception it was not something that related to me. I just did whatever I liked doing, and tried my best not to get caught by my parents. Then, when it pleased God to do so, the Holy Spirit touched my heart to reveal Christ *in me*, and I became a new creation *in Christ*. From that general timeframe forward, I grew ever more sensitive to personal sin *in my life* and that made me increasingly miserable. To be clear, I didn't set out to make this happen; it just did. I can assure you that feeling miserable was not on my "to do" list! Who would ever make it their priority to become increasingly miserable because of the sins they committed on a daily basis? My agenda was much different. I wanted just enough God to get me into heaven without robbing me of the fun I wanted to have in this life. After all, my assumption that giving yourself fully to God would be dull beyond imagining is correct—isn't it? In hindsight, God had other (and far more exciting and satisfying) plans for me.

I read John 10:10, where Jesus said, "I came that they may have life, and have it abundantly," but the only thing *abundant* in my life during these first decades of Christian living was *abundant* guilt and *abundant* condemnation. In those days, as a result of all of this guilt and self-condemnation, I frequently questioned whether I was saved at all. Now, ask yourself: In the face of such liberating verses as those mentioned above, why did I feel guilty and condemned to the point where I mentally questioned my own salvation? It was because I held a *presupposition* about the *source of sin* in my life. When I was caught up in some sinful thought or action, I believed that *I was the source* (or the "cause") of the sin (the "result" or "effect") in my life. For me, sin was simply the *product of me* the sinner. *I* was the one with the free will to make the choice to either sin or not, so when I did sin, *I* was the one to blame. *I* was the one who stood guilty and condemned before God. That thought made me thoroughly miserable. This *presupposition* led me to discount the liberating good news of Christ's once-for-all dealing with sin on the cross. The only thing left for me was misery.

But God eventually led me to realize that this *presupposition* (which I held as absolute truth) was actually not scriptural. The Apostle Paul tells us the truth of the matter in Romans 7:7–25. Using himself as the example within a step-by-step logical argument, Paul concludes that he is *not* the source of sin, but that sin is sourced from his flesh, and that the two are different from one another. He declares his own testimony that when he finds himself doing the very things he hates *(Romans 7:15), it is no longer him doing it,* but sin in his flesh *(Romans 7:17–18).*

Then he asks one of the most significant questions in the New Testament: "Wretched man that I am! *Who will set me [Paul] free from the body of this death?" (Romans 7:24).* Take a moment and personalize this verse to yourself. Swap out Paul's name for your own and read the question again. Who is going to set *YOU* free?

Paul immediately gives the answer to his own question in the next verse, but before I share that answer with you, here is what I used to think when I read Romans 7:7–25. I came to this reading with a pair of *presuppositions*: First, as I just shared, that *I was the source of* the sins I committed; and by implication from the first, that *I was also responsible* in some way with cleaning up my life so I didn't sin so much. If I had been Paul, I would have answered his question from the previous verse like this: "Now, therefore, you must strive more earnestly to bring your flesh under submission to God for His glory, which is your reasonable service to Him."

But is that what Paul answered in verse 25? Not at all! He gave all the praise and thanks to God for doing it. He said, *"Thanks be to God through Jesus Christ our Lord!* So then, on the one hand I myself with my mind am serving the law of God, but on the other, with my flesh the law of sin."

Under the inspiration of the Holy Spirit, Paul had the perfect opportunity to include himself (and us) in that "sin-dealing" equation somewhere, either by direct reference or by inference, but he did neither. Paul told us that since our sin-infested flesh (and not us) is the source of sin in our lives, *we are also not responsible* for dealing with that sin. There is only *one* source of delivery from the sin dwelling in our flesh: and that one source *is God through Jesus Christ our Lord.* "Greater is He who is in you than he who is in the world" *(1 John 4:4).* That means, in practical terms, that Christ in your spirit is greater than the demonic influences of Satan emanating from your flesh.

Only Christ's sinless nature (which has become *our* new nature as Christians), living within us as our sovereign Lord, can deal with the sin in our flesh. No part of our human effort is strong enough to deal with our own flesh; and as previously discussed, we certainly cannot deal with our flesh through any means that has been devised by our flesh. As God leads us to understand the reality of Paul's statement, we realize that this makes a gargantuan difference to the life of every Christian. From God's perspective, He sees us and sin as separate things, and He alone has the power to deal with the remaining shadow of sin in our flesh. It is not our job to engage in this clean-up campaign on our own.

God has granted us liberty, not a license to sin.
I am often confronted by concerns that such liberty may be dangerous because it seems only logical that so much liberty would give a believer the feeling that they have a license to sin. I thought the same thing for so many years

that I truly empathize with those who express this worry. This cautionary concern seems logical, as far as it goes, but closer examination exposes that it is based on a *false presupposition*: the assumption that we have the same nature *after* our salvation than we had *before* Christ came to abide in us. It presumes that if humanity has the choice, it will always choose to sin rather than prefer to do righteousness. This, of course, was entirely true for all of us prior to God revealing His Son in us. Our old nature gave no thought to God and was always predisposed to choose sin over anything else. But what happened when Christ came into us and gave us His new sinless nature? Scripture tells us that our old nature has been crucified with Christ and no longer lives, but that Christ now lives in us *(Galatians 2:20)*. We have been made into a new creation in Christ *(2 Corinthians 5:17 NIV)*.

For many years I looked at these verses and acknowledged the undeniable truth in them, while at the same time failing to actually understand the liberating implications that such truth proclaimed. I held to my *presupposition* that I was the same sinner *after* my salvation as I was *before* my salvation encounter (albeit, now I was saved by grace). In my mind, I still had a free will to choose sin or righteousness, and I chose sin far more than I wanted to admit. I gave no thought or credence to what should have been obvious to me: the life-changing power that would *naturally* result from Christ's life living within me as *my new nature*.

People are often confused by these terms "old nature" and "new nature." Let me give you an analogy to show how these terms affect our Christian living. Think of our old nature and new nature as our disposition to do certain things. Take, for example, a young lamb and a young boy who are outside frolicking about and playing all day. When it comes time to eat, they are both hungry. They both have a free will to choose what they want to eat, so let's test their individual choices. Put in front of them four options: a pile of hay, a bowl of hard oats, a grilled hotdog on a bun with ketchup, and a bowl of hot macaroni and cheese. The lamb, exercising her free will, will always choose either the hay or the hard oats over the hotdog and mac n' cheese. But the boy will choose the hotdog or mac n' cheese over eating the hay and hard oats. Are they automatons with no free choice? No, they could choose whatever they want from the four selections, but they exercise their free will *in alignment with their dispositional natures.*

This is the same with us. Prior to Christ, we lived by the *old nature* we inherited from Adam, with its disposition to choose *self-focused* things over *God-focused* things. We exercised our free will, of course, but that free will always made decisions in alignment with our old, dispositional nature. But then God revealed His Son in us *(Galatians 1: 15–16)* and Christ's life within became our *new nature.* With our old nature dead and buried, and our will unshackled from the bondage of sin and death, our human will was for the first time in our lives truly free to begin making decisions in alignment with this new dispositional nature, choosing God-directed things over sin-directed things. And when our flesh intermittently ensnared us into doing sinful things, like Paul, we hated it. It made us miserable. It would be like making that little boy eat hard oats and hay for dinner.

By now, I hope you are beginning to see why it is impossible for Christ's life in us to ever give us a license to sin. If we continued on, after our salvation, with our old nature still in place, then yes, we would be giving people a license to sin because that is precisely what they would choose to do. They would make decisions *in alignment* with their old, dispositional nature. But that is *not* the good-news reality of what God has given us as our salvation. He has crucified and buried our old nature with Christ *(Galatians 2:20)*, and replaced our *old nature* with Christ within us as our *new nature.* We don't have two natures, but one. That new nature directs our free-will decisions *in alignment* with its desire for more God-things. That is why we think of God, choose to pray to Him, read our Bibles, seek fellowship with other believers, go to church, and so on. We are making free-will decisions *in alignment with our new nature in Christ.* We have nothing to boast of here; it is all God!

He made us vessels of mercy, not partners.
Can you handle some more good news? Our part in God's plan is not as a partner, but as a vessel of mercy to contain His glory, a glory that God reveals in us when it pleases Him *(Galatians 1:15–16)*. A glory that increasingly grows *in us* from glory to glory as God gently and progressively performs His work in us *(2 Corinthians 3:18)*. We are His workmanship *(Ephesians 2:10)*, as clay in the Potter's hands *(Romans 9:20–21)*. And He continues to do His divine will and work, according to His good pleasure, throughout our lives *(Philippians 1:6, 2:13)*. He has placed us on His ever-brightening path of righteousness *(Proverbs 4:18)* where

He is bringing us to a place where we trust Him for everything *(Proverbs 3:5–6)*.

What is the common theme in all of these verses? *God is the one* who is actively working in our lives, and we are either the "vessel," or the "clay," or the "object" being transformed from glory to glory. I could list hundreds of verses just like the verses above. In my earlier years as a Christian, I had little problem accepting all of the above scripture as fact. The problem for me was not in the facts themselves, but in how the obvious *implications* from these verses were in direct conflict with all of my *presuppositions* about what the verses meant. If all of these facts are true, then to my earthly logic, it *removed me* from the equation of Christian discipleship and discipline. This human logic led me to cybernate between either *discounting* the clear meaning of these verses, or *disbelieving* the verses entirely. Of course, I would never admit to disbelieving a verse, but my actions reflected that disbelief. How can it be true that *God has done it all and He is all we need*? We must have some part to play as disciples of the Christ—true? Well, not so fast. Being a "disciple" has nothing to do with whether we are the ones responsible for dealing with sin in our lives. This concept is another false *presupposition* that robs us of God's liberating freedom in our daily lives, whether at work or at home.

God gave us an *all-inclusive* salvation!
Take for an example, our understanding of God's gift of personal salvation. Most Christians readily acknowledge that their salvation was entirely an act of God's mercy and grace. The circumstances differed, but the essence of the life-giving gift was the same: By the Holy Spirit's loving

touch, we recognized our condition, that we were dead in our trespasses and sins *(Ephesians 2:1)*, and came to believe in God's gift of salvation through His Son Jesus. Most of us also readily recognize that God is actively working in their lives, although some doubt and worry about this.

The hard part for the human mind to comprehend (and our religious flesh to accept) is the fact that the very same salvation that we so readily accept as *completely from God* is also actually *all-inclusive*. It includes *everything* we need for living our day-to-day lives on earth prior to glory. To say this in a different way: *God's gift of salvation is already perfect and complete*. There is no need for us to add anything to it—to cooperate, coordinate or capitulate to God, or to partner with Him, or help Him in any way. It is *all-inclusive* because this wonderful gift of salvation from God is filled to the brim with vastly more than we ever imagined as included in this solitary gift.

One way to consider this term "salvation" is to think of it as sort of an *umbrella* term that covers the gamut of God's blessings for us. It not only includes *redemption* (what we think of as our salvation), but also total *sanctification* (what we think of as spiritual growth) and complete *righteousness*, as well as His moment-by-moment divine *wisdom* to guide us through each day *(1 Corinthians 1:30)*. God's gift of salvation, then, is not just a "ticket to get into heaven" when we die, but includes an interim transfer-token from the kingdom of darkness into the kingdom of His Son, right now, and in this life.

How is this possible? Read 1 Corinthians 1:30–31 *without any presuppositions* and the answer is obvious: "But by His doing [God's doing, not ours] you are in Christ Jesus, who became to us wisdom from God, and righteousness and sanctification, and redemption, so that, just as it is written, 'LET HIM WHO BOASTS, BOAST IN THE LORD.'" All of this perfect salvation was given to us, not as a set of terms to stash away in our religious lexicon, but as a *person* who lives His life *in us*—Christ Jesus our Lord and Savior. This is the *best way* to think about our salvation—as the *person* of Christ Jesus living His life in us. Everything we need to live our lives is all included in Him. Are you facing an urgent crisis or problem in your life? Christ can never be stumped over any problem. A situation may come upon us suddenly and surprise us, but He saw its arrival from before the foundation of the world and has prepared a path of peace for us to travel through it. We are but vessels to contain His glory *(Romans 9:23)*.

What, then, is left for us to do?
The honest answer from scripture is: NOTHING! But that doesn't mean you will be a couch-potato or some sort of passive do-nothing vegetable. The real answer to this question is natural, organic, and far simpler than we would ever imagine. The complexity of today's lifestyle tends to obfuscate the essence of what being a *disciple of the Christ* really means. Let me explain.

Read any one of the four gospels, or all of them, paying special attention to the disciples that the Lord called to follow him. Think of those disciples as the model for what it is for us to be disciples today. What did they do? They followed Jesus around wherever He decided to go; they asked Him questions and listened when He spoke to them; they conversed with Him in give-and-take conversations;

they attended the gatherings that the Lord decided to go to; they discussed among themselves what the Lord meant by certain comments He made; and they witnessed *firsthand* the Lord's miracles over nature, over disease, and even over death. In other words, they did what the Lord told Joshua to do (they spent their lives in the Lord's presence, walking on holy ground [*see* chapter two]).

Were they couch-potatoes? Of course not, and no one throughout church history has ever suggested that they were. They were as busy as the Lord was because they were following Him throughout the regions of Palestine and Judea. The one thing that consumed their lives, from morning until night, was staying in the presence of Jesus. They didn't go off to their jobs as fishermen or tax collectors during the day and only followed Jesus at night or on the weekends. Jesus was their full-time passion. But they were always as busy (or not) as Jesus decided to be at any particular time. When Jesus paused by the Jordan River, they baptized people coming to Him to the point where they were baptizing more people than John the Baptist. That sounds like a great ministry, but did they argue when Jesus suddenly (to their perception) decided to leave this all behind and travel through Samaria? No, they just stopped baptizing and continued following Him. They had a simple life, focused on Christ. Of course, we read in scripture that Jesus wasn't making a sudden decision at all. Jesus had an appointment with a Samaritan woman by the well at noonday from before the foundation of the world, and He was not going to be late for it.

Now, to be clear, I am not suggesting that the disciples were perfect. Far from it! Scripture is clear that they had all the frailties that we have. They showed cowardice at times and were frightened. They repeatedly demonstrated their lack of faith. They denied Him at times and took their eyes off Him at times. In other words, they generally did not recognize or understand who Jesus was, or the scope of His divine mission, until Pentecost. My point here is this: in spite of their frailties and lack of understanding, John 17 verses 11 and 12 tell us that Christ kept them protected. He did not lose a single one, but Judas, the son of perdition, so that scripture would be fulfilled. These men were faithful disciples, not because of their own wisdom and insight, but because God had given them into Christ's hand.

Ask yourself: Where else would these disciples want to be? He had the words of eternal life. What else would they want to do? Would owning the wealthiest fishing enterprise in the region satisfy them now that they had come face to face with Jesus? There was no place, other than in the Lord's presence, where they wanted to be. At one point, Jesus gave them some specific instructions before sending them out to heal the sick throughout the region. They followed His leading and at that point performed miracles in His name, but they didn't set out to do this on their own, nor is there any record of them doing so again until after Pentecost. They were sent by Jesus for a specific purpose and length of time before returning to Him and continuing in His presence to follow Him.

The simple truth is: We are no different than those early disciples, except that we have been called by God into a life of discipleship after Christ's death and resurrection. Now we have Christ Jesus living *in us* as our Great Shepherd!

You might say that we are more intimately in the Lord's presence than those early disciples were.

So when someone asks me: "What is left for me to do?"

I say: "Just *recognize* that you live your life in the presence of the *How-Great-Thou-Art* Almighty God, on the *holy ground* that He has placed you on. You can trust Him for everything. In fact, you don't even need to come up with your own trust; He will provide that to you as well, precisely when you need it. Prayer and scripture are also powerful gifts from Him, but He'll bring the desire to pray, and a hunger for His word, or a specific verse to mind precisely when you need it. He will direct your path every day of your life *(Proverbs 20:24)*."

As you go through your day, you are living your life as a citizen *in* Christ's kingdom. You don't *try* to live your life in Christ's kingdom; you just do because God has transferred you there. You get up each morning *in* Christ's kingdom, you travel to work *in* His kingdom; you make that phone call or attend that business meeting *in* His kingdom, everywhere you go throughout your day, you are always *in* His kingdom. This means, whether you are consciously aware of it or not, the King is directing your path; He is working within you, both to will and to work His good pleasure and to transform you from glory to glory. These are His promises direct from scripture, without *presuppositions* or equivocations. If you think back over your life, even during the hardest of times, you can see how God was caring for you and protecting you. God has always taken care of you (and me) through every challenge and hardship.

I know that this doesn't make our religious flesh comfortable because we feel like we should be actively involved and doing something. I know it also challenges dozens of *presuppositions* we hold as part of our effort to live a victorious Christian life. But the truth is still the truth. The only thing left to be done in our remaining days on earth is *for Christ* to live His life out in us *for God's glory*. It is not our job to live Christ's life out in us. That's impossible for us to accomplish. Only Christ can live His divine life out in us. We are but vessels of mercy to contain His glory. There is *nothing* left to do that any human can boast about *(1 Corinthians 1:31)*. If you had something to do, some part to play in partnership with God, would you not then have something to boast about because of your efforts? But scripture says that man has nothing to boast in, save but God. This is the word of God and worthy of our acceptance.

Think of it this way. One morning, a few years ago, I was engaged in my daily four-mile run, when I began to feel a dull pain in my chest. It wasn't so painful that I stopped running, but it definitely was not normal. Back at the house, Sherryl called my doctor, who wanted me to go to the hospital for some tests. Within a couple of hours I was undergoing emergency quadruple bypass heart surgery.

Now ask yourself: Did I have anything to do with conducting the heart surgery which saved my life that day? Of course, not! I had lost all ability to help myself in any way. It was the medical team of physicians and nurses that deserve this credit. This is analogous to God's working in us. It is entirely His doing and we have no partnership in it.

But look at this same surgery from another perspective: Was I only a couch-potato and an uninterested bystander to this surgery? The answers to that question is also no. I certainly had no partnership in the surgery itself, but I

have the long scars on my chest to prove that I fully partici-
pated in it. I had the pain following surgery to live through
and the rehabilitation that comes with such surgery. God's
spiritual surgery on us is no different. When I say that we
have nothing to do that aids or assists God's working in us,
that is purely a factual matter. It does not mean that we are
not "front and center" in living our lives. We do experience
the *results* of His working in us. Sometimes that can bring
temporary pain, but it always brings us to greater peace
and spiritual health in our life.

Does that sound too good to be true?

Yet another *presupposition* that often keeps us from experiencing God's total freedom in Christ is the notion that:
If it sounds too good to be true, then it probably isn't true. The
danger in this assumption is that when it comes to earthly
matters this saying is often more true than not, but that
doesn't mean it is *always* true. Especially when it comes to
God; because His ways and thoughts are not our ways and
thoughts *(Isaiah 55:8–9)*, so when we tap into the truths of
God in scripture, they *always* seem too good to be true to
our human thinking.

Keep in mind that of all the beliefs and religions in the
world, true Christianity is unique. No other religion can
compare to it on many levels. The Apostle Paul describes
the "good news" he preached to the Galatians as a gospel of
freedom and liberty. Throughout the New Testament, the
Christian life is referred to as being "light," "easy," "restful," *(Matthew 11:29–30)*, with a goal of "freedom" *(Galatians
5:1)*. It is also referred to by various inspired writers as

"peaceful" *(Hebrews 12:11),* "simple" *(2 Corinthians 11:3),* and "not burdensome" *(1 John 5:3–4).*

But our lives are often filled with heart-breaking pain from illness or the loss of a loved one. It is filled with periods of being out of work or laboring at a job we hate so we can put food on the table for our kids. During your life, you may be called upon to slog through the collapse of your business, with divorce, with rebellious children, with drug addictions, or spousal infidelity. Remember, God transferred us *out* of the kingdom of darkness, but not out of the world *(John 17:15).* While we endure the flaming arrows from the world, we remain safe in the kingdom of His Son. That is what Psalm 23 is all about:

1 *The Lord is my shepherd,*
  I shall not want.
2 *He makes me lie down in green pastures;*
  He leads me beside quiet waters.
3 *He restores my soul;*
  He guides me in the paths of righteousness
  For His name's sake.
4 *Even though I walk through the valley of the shadow of death,*
  I fear no evil, for You are with me;
  Your rod and Your staff, they comfort me.
5 *You prepare a table before me in the presence of my enemies;*
  You have anointed my head with oil;
  My cup overflows.
6 *Surely goodness and lovingkindness will follow me all*
  the days of my life,
  And I will dwell in the house of the LORD *forever.*

When you read this Psalm, does it not resonate with King David's personal experience of what it meant for him to walk about in God's kingdom? King David didn't speak only of a hunky-dory life where there are no problems. On the contrary, he speaks of being in the presence of his enemies and of journeying through the shadow of death, but those are not the foci of the Psalm. King David's focus was on his Shepherd, not on his problems. As such, he felt no fear, but was comforted and felt that his cup was overflowing with goodness and lovingkindness from God all the days of his life. We learn from King David that God doesn't promise us a life free of problems—*but one that is full of peace*—even in the midst of those problems. Read the Psalm again carefully. Can you find any suggestion that we have some part to play while being shepherded by God? We have the Lord as our Shepherd. He guides and protects us. Even though we walk through the shadows of death, we fear no evil for He is with us. Our only boast is the Lord as our Shepherd; we shall not want.

Give us an example of Christ as your Shepherd.
I have spoken to many groups about what it truly means (to me) to be a successful Christian businessman. Inevitably, someone will come up after the meeting and ask for specific examples of how I used to act versus how I act now. I often gave them one or more verses that have meant so much to me during my business life (some of which I have included as a potpourri collection in the back of this book). I know these questions are well intended, but they are really fishing for a set of steps or a formula of five or ten points that they can then attempt to apply to their own lives. That is

something I can't give them because I don't have the mind of God for what He is doing uniquely in each of their lives. I know for certain that He is doing it, but I don't know what He is doing or what the timing is for His doing it. Such advice, if I tried to give it, would be nothing more than my earthly wisdom in running a business. To answer in this way would turn this testimony into a self-help book. That would probably sell more books, but it wouldn't deliver truth from scripture that leads to true peace and success in business or in life.

I can, however, give you an example of what I mean when I say that God is working in us and transforming us, often without our knowing it (at the time), or even being aware of it. That may allow you to prayerfully look back on your life to see a similar pattern of transformation within your own heart.

Take for example the question: *Are you an honest person?*

If someone had asked me that question 30 years ago, I would have been perplexed as to why such a question was being asked of me. I think my first response would have been measured and disciplined, like: "Am I honest? Yes, I believe I'm honest." But my thoughts would be racing: *I was practically born that way. My father was a preacher; I grew up in a Christian home and even graduated from a four-year Bible college. Today I'm a Sunday-school teacher and elder in my church, as well as a tax-paying citizen and a faithful husband. Honesty is part of who I am.*

Obviously, from this answer, you can readily discern the nature of what I thought honesty was in those days. Somehow, I got in my mind the frivolous notion that honesty is *a set of outward activities* (or a way of performing external tasks) that makes the person honest. If I could manage to act in a certain way, this made me honest. At the time, I thought no more deeply about it than that. Had I been a betting man, I would have bet money that honesty was the *last thing* that God needed to work on *in me*. In my mind, I was perfectly fine the way I was.

I was wrong.

God had other plans and He would not require my help in accomplishing those plans.

Lying to my wife.
"When will you be home tonight?" Sherryl would ask.

"Six o'clock *sharp*," I would reply, purposely emphasizing the word *sharp*.

This was a typical telephone conversation I had with my wife almost every day. Sherryl would call about midday to coordinate the evening meal to be ready when I got home. That way I could eat a hot meal and spend time with the kids as a family. For my part, I knew she wanted me to say six o'clock, so I said six o'clock. I would answer whatever I thought she wanted the answer to be.

Of course, I typically arrived home much later than that, usually citing the excuse that something "important" unexpectedly came up at work. I wasn't completely insensitive, of course. I could tell that Sherryl was upset by this behavior every time it happened (which was several times a week), but I always managed to justify it to myself: *After all, I'm not late because I was goofing off; the business needed my attention. I'm only trying to provide a better life for her and the family. Isn't tending shop what every good Christian husband should do?* Preoccupied with these self-justifying thoughts, it never occurred to me that not keeping my word to Sherryl was actually being dishonest with her. Had I stopped a moment to think about it, I would never have considered it an option to make an appointment with a customer or colleague, with the hidden attitude that I could show up an hour or two late with impunity. But that was different, right?

Arriving home one evening, late as usual, I found my dinner plate in its familiar spot on the kitchen counter, ready to be heated again in the microwave. The kids were long gone to bed. I placed the plate in the microwave just as Sherryl came into the kitchen. It wasn't long before she was reminding me *again* how much she wished I could make it home on time so I could have a hot meal with the family. Now, here is how self-centered I was and oblivious to almost everything going on around me. I perceived that Sherryl was communicating an unhappiness that *I* had to eat reheated leftovers for dinner when I came home late, so I said:

"It doesn't bother me to eat…"

"Daryl," she cut across my developing excuse, and spoke in a near whisper from a place of anguish in her heart, "it may not be important for you to eat a hot meal with me and the kids, *but it's important to me.*" With that, she walked out of the kitchen and left me alone.

Looking back, had Sherryl made similar comments to me before? Of course, scores of times. It certainly was not in her power to change me. None of her comments ever penetrated my self-absorbed world until that night. For the first time, I finally heard that it wasn't about *me*—it was about *the family* I claimed to love. For some reason on that particular night, my self-justifying excuses didn't kick in fast enough to shield me from the truth Sherryl had spoken in a voice barely above the hum of the microwave. Was this enlightenment of my own doing? That is a laughable thought. The last thing I thought was that I needed to change. The only source of this clarity was from God's working in me. That night, He touched a deaf man's ears so he could finally hear what needed to be heard.

Was I miraculously changed overnight?

No. I had completely forgotten about it by the next morning.

But then the following week, the Lord directed my attention to Psalm 15:1–2:

> O Lord, who may abide in Your tent?
> Who may dwell on Your holy hill?
> He who *walks with integrity*...
> And **speaks truth in his heart**.

As is so often the case, we come to the word of God with our own agenda, but God has other plans. In this case, I was rushing to prepare a Sunday-school lesson; but the word of God is living and operative and sharper than any two-edged sword *(Hebrews 4:12)*. God wanted to open my understanding to something much dearer to Him than a Sunday-school lesson. The instant I started to read this verse, before I had finished the first line, the Lord powerfully flooded into my memory the words that Sherryl had spoken to me the previous week. He began to shed light on my deceptive conduct regarding that whole situation. I realized from God that I had been dealing with my wife solely on an external level, telling her what I thought she wanted to hear, regardless of whether I actually intended to keep my word. I never thought to look beyond the superficial of what I was saying and doing, to what was really *in my heart.*

God was shedding His light on the *real* problem—the *impurity* residing in my heart. The truth was: I didn't consider being home with my family at 6:00 p.m. a big deal. As a matter of fact, I didn't consider *any* of my commitments to my wife and kids to be on the same level of importance as my work. It is hardly surprising, then, that deceptive communications and hurtful actions flowed from these *impure* attitudes *in my heart*; and I repeatedly made and broke commitments to my family on countless occasions. Before God touched my heart that day, I was blind to the truth of the matter: that I wasn't being honest with my wife and family concerning my intentions—right from that midday telephone call.

As I read Psalm 15, the Lord made it painfully clear to me that He desires for *all* my words and actions to reflect *His* truth. What I spoke with my mouth needed to be consistent with what I believed in my heart; and what my heart believed needed to be consistent with the truth revealed in God's word. Regardless of whom I was addressing, I was to be centered not on what I thought others wanted to hear or what I felt comfortable saying, but purely on *the integrity of my word.*

Even then, was I one hundred percent transformed in that moment of reading Psalm 15 to *always* tell the truth to my wife? No. That isn't how God usually works His deeper truths into me. It took more episodes and more scripture. But over time, the Holy Spirit touched my heart and enabled me to *truly listen* to Sherryl and understand *why* that daily family meal was so important to her. When I understood her perspective, I was ashamed of my shallowness; and the value of those meal times grew more important to me.

Again, by the Holy Spirit's gentle touch, I connected emotionally with just how much hurt my absence and self-centeredness had caused my wife for so many years. At first, the conviction of this knowledge was crushing and I closed my eyes and turned from it. But as God continued to penetrate my heart more deeply with His truth, the heaviness I felt gave way to relief—to an entirely new heart priority. For the first time, I experienced a genuine desire to keep my word to my wife; I *wanted* to arrange my schedule according to that 6:00 p.m. gathering with Sherryl and the kids. And not so surprisingly, I quickly learned that keeping that appointment was not as onerous a task as I had once thought it to be.

I soon became aware that not every issue at work was a "crisis" requiring my immediate attention. For example, if a staff member dropped in around 4:30 with a problem, or an associate called at the end of the day to ask for advice, I felt at liberty (for the first time in my business life) to weigh the seriousness of the issue before immediately jumping into the fray. I would ask myself: What is my best estimate of how long this will take to resolve? Is this matter something that will jeopardize customer confidence? Is it *truly* time-sensitive? Or can it wait until the next business day with no negative consequences?

As it turned out, once I started asking these questions, most of these so-called urgent concerns, that previously kept me working late at night, were just as easily and effectively handled in the morning. In fact, allowing these non-urgent matters to wait overnight often resulted in more thoughtful and peaceful solutions to the problem. It didn't take long for others in the company to apply these same questions to the problems they faced before escalating the matter to me. That reduced even further those things coming to my desk late in the day.

And in those rare instances when an emergency truly did present itself, the Lord touched my heart to develop the habit of calling Sherryl *first* to let her know I'd be late. I would set up a new time when I would be home during that call, which I made a priority to keep.

Each of these insights did not come all at once, but flowed from *God's progressive working in my heart*. Sometimes God's working in our hearts can be painful, but we read in Hebrews 12:11, "All discipline for the moment seems not to be joyful, but sorrowful; yet to those who have been trained by it, afterwards it yields the peaceful fruit of righteousness." This verse is truly my experience with regards to my dishonesty to Sherryl and our kids. Notice that the *discipline* in this verse is not for punishment, but for *training*. It is our loving Father's dealing with impurity in our hearts and His training us up in His righteous way. This is what Proverbs 4:18 is talking about: "But the path of the righteous is like the light of dawn, that shines brighter and brighter until the full day." We didn't put ourselves on this path, God did. He is also the One who draws us along this path to see and experience His righteousness as an ever-brightening light in our hearts.

Chapter Seven:

Bottom-Line Perspective

(The "X" Factor: God instills a passion for knowing Him)

> *"Let them give thanks to the LORD for His loving-kindness...! For He has satisfied the thirsty soul, and the hungry soul He has filled with what is good."*
>
> PSALM 107:8—9

What makes Environment Control (our company), or any company, different?

I have considered this question repeatedly over the years. Whenever an employee tells me that "this is a peaceful place to work" or a vendor comes into the office and comments, "Wow, this place is different," it often draws me to ponder: *What is it that people find so different?*

Of course, I've asked a few of them directly. Some say that it's the *sense of peace* that permeates the office complex. But for me, that is a *manifestation* rather than a *cause*. I wanted to know what *causes* the peace in the first place. Others surmise that it's because I am a Christian. But in my mind, there are tens of thousands of businesses out there owned by Christians, and in reality, every Christian has the same Christ in them. This *alone* cannot be the reason.

Nor can it be that our policies within the company are more spiritual or outwardly religious. We are the opposite. We do have two discreet Bible verses, on each end of the building—one located at the base of a granite sculpture of two swans, and the other inscribed within a painted wall mural of a landscape scene—but that's the only thing visible to the public. We never raise the issue of faith or Christianity at any time during our job interviews with prospective employees. Being a Christian is *not* a job requirement at Environment Control. We focus entirely on the specific job qualifications required for the position we are looking to fill. We do give every finalist candidate advanced notice that the company was (and is) founded on a deeply held Christian heritage, but that's as far as it goes.

So, what makes Environment Control different? Or any other company in a similar position?

Is it because we have taken special care to hire good people over the years?

Is it because our office building is nestled in a grove of evergreen trees?

Is it because we are located in a smaller resort community, away from the hustle and bustle of a major metropolitan city?

While all of these things are true, none of them, individually or in combination, appear to be the cause of *what makes Environment Control a truly special place to work.* From my own perspective, with the exception of a few odd jobs in high school and my early college days, I've always worked *only* at Environment Control. So, I have no point of reference to know the veracity of these observations from others, one way or the other; but I respect the scores of people who have told me that this is so. Regardless of the reason, I have no boast—since I did absolutely nothing to make it happen this way. Up until recently, the unanswered question remained: What makes it so?

I haven't had a satisfactory explanation for this phenomenon until just the last few months. The topic came up serendipitously at the conclusion of a meeting with one of our corporate transactional attorneys. I asked him how he felt the company was doing overall. It was an open-ended question to spur a general opinion from this corporate professional, now that he had worked with the company as his client for several years. Admittedly, the question was outside the scope of why he had been engaged by the company in the first place, but while I had the face-to-face opportunity, I wanted to learn if there were any specific suggestions for corporate governance or operational improvements that he might offer.

He said, "I wouldn't change a thing. This place is unique."

Here we go again, I thought; someone else is commenting on this elusive sense of "difference" that the company seems to exude; but I asked, "How so?"

He said, "Well, I'm just an observer here, but I've worked with hundreds of corporate clients during my legal practice, from IBM and Boeing on the large end, to as small as a one-man shop or a company with less than a dozen employees. This company is unique...and I mean that in a positive way. You make a modest profit, but you aren't obsessed with making money or your bottom line like most companies, which tells me that the company is governed by a different set of values. Do you understand what I'm saying?"

"Not really," I said. "This topic of being different or unique does come up from time to time. People often comment on how *peaceful* the office environment is. But frankly, we've never been able to explain it or pin the source of it down. We DO care about the bottom line, though, or we wouldn't still be in business after fifty years. After all, if you don't run a business in a way to make money, you won't be in business for long. And if you don't keep your focus on that earned dollar, then it slips away before you know it. So, I do focus on profit. In fact, I would say we are quite meticulous about it. I never lose sight of it. I know what's happening in the corporation every day and I'm translating that information, along with sales reports, financial statements, etc., into planning that affects the bottom line, cash flow, profit, all of it."

"No question there, Daryl. I can see all of that by working with you. But there's a difference between *being obsessed* with the bottom line and being a *responsible steward* of the bottom line. Do you understand that difference?"

"Oh, yeah, I lived most of my life on the obsessive side of that equation."

"Good, then you know from experience what I'm talking about. I wasn't referring to the *diligent stewardship* of the bottom line, which every business needs to do, but I was referring to the fact that the company doesn't appear *obsessed* over it."

"Okay, that's definitely true."

"Most successful companies stay on top of their finances as you do. There is nothing unique or different about your company from that perspective. What I'm actually talking about is something that may affect the operational bottom line, but occurs at a much deeper level within a company. I could think about this more and possibly come up with a better way to say this, but here's a short take-away for you.

"In my opinion, what you want to know is not rocket science. It's a rather straight-forward, 'cause-and-effect' dynamic. If you were doing a systems analysis of your company, the answer to your question would likely show up as the most foundational *systemic process* that takes place *within* your company. As I say, there's nothing unique about it in and of itself; you just have to identify it. Think of the tranquility and *peacefulness* that people comment on as an *end result* of this *systemic process*. An environment of peace doesn't just happen by accident. It's produced as a *product* of a *systemic process* established within this corporation. I don't know who first coined the concept, but it's a favorite saying among my engineering clients: 'Every system is perfectly designed to produce the result it yields.' A system is a collective grouping of many independent elements—people, practices, policies, and procedures—that all synergistically collaborate and interact to produce a cohesive goal—in this case: peace. What would you consider to be your company's most foundational *systemic process*?"

"I'd have to think about that for a while."

"Well, that's why you're puzzled by the resulting peace in your office. It's a product of a process that you aren't yet aware of."

"But we don't have any policies or goals that set out to produce peace in our office. You can't just make a rule that says: 'Peace shall permeate the office at all times—or the offender will be fired!'"

"True enough!" he laughed, "but I didn't say anything about policies, goals, or rules. Those are all *products* of the same *systemic process* that peace is produced from. Think of it this way: People conceptualize corporations, or any business entity for that matter, as inanimate legal constructs, as though the building we are sitting in here at Environment Control with the sign out front, is the corporation. It's not. *The essence of every business is people.* Big companies have a lot of people, small companies have a few people, but the *commonality* between *all* companies regardless of their size or what business they engage in, is their collective tribe of *people,* some refer to it as their *family,* who work together within the company.

"Within various corporations, the people at the senior executive level are motivated by different things. Some are consumed with dominating the niche market where the company operates, others are entirely focused on competition, or growth, or various forms of expansion like gobbling up other companies through the merger and acquisition process, and still others zero in on bottom-line profit to the exclusion of everything else; or for others: how the public perceives them in terms of quality, value, or price. To use an analogy here, this motivating force in the hearts of these senior executives is like the wind that blows in the 'corporate tree' that makes the leaves move. Every leaf is an employee that moves in a collective unison because of this unseen force that drives them all in the same direction, toward the same goal.

"This motivation, of course, is often *not* recognized because it is hidden within the hearts of senior management and is not expressed openly—just as the wind is not seen but can be deduced from the movement of the leaves. Now, corporations put all manner of labels on this dynamic. For public consumption, they might call it a 'corporate vision' or 'statement of values' or 'corporate purpose.' Internal to the corporation, they may speak of it more frankly as strategic or tactical planning, objectives, targets, goals, or whatever.

"Deeper still, however, is what resides in the heart of the senior executive officer of the corporation. Is his or her compensation tied to certain objective criteria or some specified set of metrics? If so, these hidden motivators (along with any natural inclination that this executive might have toward being greedy or competitive) may secretly be setting the agenda (that is to say, creating the impetus for the *systemic process* I'm talking about) from a place that no one else is aware of. Of course, this executive officer will craft and communicate his or her goals in a way that will sound less self-serving, but however these essential goals are characterized or classified, they become the animating spirit, the *passion* if you will, that gives the collective family its sense of purpose and direction. It is this *passion* that brings life to the corporate workplace and stirs people to action. It's what animates the corporation with living energy. It's the wind blowing the leaves on the tree. It's the life-force that eventually ends up (at the other end of the *systemic process*) producing a working environment that each employee experiences every day when they come to work—an environment of agitation, pressure, and stress, or one of tranquility, serenity, and peace. The former gets every employee addicted to their own adrenaline, while the latter, for the most part, is free of it.

"What makes this organization different, Daryl, is that it doesn't appear to be motivated by any of the things I just mentioned, which is a list that covers about 90% of all motivations in business. Only you know what's in your heart. Only you can speak concerning your primary motivation. *What is it that you are passionate about far and above anything else in your life?* Once you figure that out, then you'll have your answer as to why your company is unique."

I sat quietly listening until he finished, and then I thanked him for his comments. I didn't carry the conversation further because I already knew what God was telling me. I knew the truth of what was being said. I knew *exactly* what that primary motivator was in my heart that set in motion everything else in my business. It had been the same since the day I stood by Dave's hospital bed decades earlier. It was back then that I prayed the most earnest prayer in my entire life. It was then when I inwardly poured myself out to God—telling Him how I could no longer go on, how I could no longer bear the weight of life, and how I didn't care about any of it any more. To be clear, this was not my salvation prayer. I had been a Christian for years by then. It was my *burned-out-from-trying-to-be-a-good-Christian-businessman* prayer. I felt stripped of everything and clung to one solitary desire:

Dear God, I just want to know You!
From that prayer until today, by the grace of God, this solitary desire has remained resident within me as my deepest heart's desire. *Every day* since that day, God has answered that heart-felt prayer in a fresh way. That's right; in 2013, I am the daily recipient of God's answer to a prayer I prayed thirty years ago! He is always drawing me to pray and read His word, always granting me a fresh dose of His passion to know only Him in my life. *Everything* pales in comparison to this. *Nothing* is as important...*nothing* comes close.

I had my answer.

Tangible peace in the workplace flows from God's peace in my heart. What makes a business special is the desire that God places in our hearts to know (experience) Him alone—just Him, only Him, and nothing but Him. I'll explain what I mean by "knowing Him" later in this chapter.

God instills a passion for His leading (through peace).
The singular desire to know only God has produced within me a passion for doing only what the Lord is doing. I am no longer driven by the bright sparkle or simmering urgency of an emerging opportunity, but care only to be led throughout each day by God's Spirit. This is not a practice you can flip-on like a light switch, but is something God grows in us day by day in a loving and patient way over the course of our lives. I don't think this is something we ever stop learning about or growing into this side of glory. It is truly God's eternal work in us—to cause us to trust Him in *everything.*

But one thing I can say, it doesn't take long, once God has turned your focus to Him alone, to remove the primary compulsion that drives you to "make money," or "expand your business," or "protect your job," or any of these other business-related, stress-producing, compulsions. That, in turn, breaks the cycle that inevitably produces stress, worry, anxiety, and pressure within each of us personally (and by extension, every other person who works in the company with us).

Once God has broken this vicious cycle, He replaces it with a more stable and positive one. We soon discover, often to our surprise, that we can actually commit whatever time is necessary to bring whatever "opportunity" or problem facing us to the Lord for *His leading.* You will find, as I did, that much of our activity in the course of a business day is not genuinely urgent or critical. The amazing fact is that most of the urgency in business is actually *self-generated* and *self-perpetuated*—based on motives we have *other than* simply to know God—rather than His Spirit peacefully directing our steps.

Let me give you an example of what I am talking about. A few years ago, we received a confidential phone call from our bank informing us of something that was not yet announced, but would soon become public. We learned that the federal government had chosen the property immediately across the street from our corporate offices in Coeur d'Alene, Idaho, for a new federal court house. The bank informed us that this was a windfall opportunity for us because properties immediately surrounding such projects were always snapped up and office buildings were built to house law firms and supporting businesses. The bank volunteered to lend us the money to purchase the land next to us and even to build a larger office complex when we so desired. Could this be an opportunity from God? I mean, how often does your bank call you to lend you money?

The more we explored this opportunity, the better it looked. We did contact the owner of the property next door to us (the same owner who had sold us our initial parcel of land). Rather than hide this confidential information from them, we shared what we knew, then asked if they would be interested in selling the adjoining parcel to us. Not only did they sell it to us, but they sold it for the same price per acre that we paid for the initial parcel some five years prior. From our human perspective, it looked like God was blessing this project!

That led us to engage an architect and formulate a design that would integrate a new larger office building next to the original corporate offices, and link them in theme and landscape into a unified campus with a large fountain system between them. The corporate office would then move to the new larger building and lease the old facility to one of the incoming law firms. During this process, we were contacted by several law firms, inquiring whether they could purchase or lease the old building from us. *Everything* related to this opportunity gave me nothing but green lights to go forward with the construction of this new office complex.

Everything, that is, with *one* exception: I did not have peace from God to move forward.

So, what did I do?

I waited. We had the land. We had the commitment of funding, and we had the architectural design. But we didn't have the peace. And for me, *no peace* outweighed everything else. In my experience, *God does not lead by opportunity—He leads by peace (Proverbs 3:17)*. There are scores of wonderful opportunities that come to my attention every year; that doesn't mean every opportunity I learn about is something that God wants for me to be involved in.

Well, no more than six months later, the bottom fell out of the economy. Other office buildings under construction, in response to this federal project, were completed and stood empty (and many of them are still empty after several years). Had I moved forward with the construction of that new building, we would have suffered a considerable financial hardship. It further would have stressed us financially into the future to a point of being uncomfortable.

I can only lift up praise to God for this result. It wasn't sage wisdom from me that saved us from this hardship. Everything pointed to the conclusion that we needed to move forward quickly with construction. Had we applied the typical business motivations, for greater company growth or higher investment returns, we would have surely gone forward. But those were not our motivations. We had only *one* motivation, and that was *to know God and be led by Him*. As it always turns out with God, He knew better. He had a clear view of the deep economic doldrums that were about to hit us and He protected us from its most dire impact.

Does this mean that we will never build this building? I don't know. Every day I look at that beautiful piece of property next to our building and thank the Lord that He will give us the peace when, or if, we are to build it. He may never give us that peace, and that would be fine. Our goal is not to construct bigger buildings, but *to know God and know His leading*. Scripture says that *all* of His paths are peace (*Proverbs 3:17*).

God instills a passion (and the skills) for good stewardship.
Perhaps you are thinking right now: *What planet do you come from, Daryl? You don't care about making money? If you're not in business to make money, then what are you in business for?*

Here lies a critical distinction that would be helpful to understand. Keep in mind, as you read this paragraph, that the deepest desire in my heart these days is *to know God and follow His leading.* This is what God has instilled within me—like the breath I breathe every day—it is the abiding passion that animates what I do and how I make decisions. This, in turn, affects every dimension of the business. With that in mind, I certainly do run the business to make money, but making money is not the *animating force* that drives me in business. *I'm* in business because God led me into this particular business (and has given me the necessary skills to run it) and has kept me here for fifty years now.

For my part, just as Joseph served as a diligent steward for the Egyptian Pharaoh, I also desire to run this business as a steward of the Most High God. I can tell you from experience that God is meticulous and detailed in all things related to business. But the motivation of *why* I am in business is entirely different than what it once was. As we discussed in chapter three, this business is a tool in God's hand to perform His work in me. While I work in this business, God is faithfully working in me (my heart). This is a deeper drumbeat than the bottom line.

As I get older, people increasingly ask me, "When are you going to retire?"

I tell them, "When God leads me to retire."

I understand why they ask the question. I'm 71 years old and have had two heart surgeries. Yet, I still come into work every day. I spend time with my sons discussing various aspects of the business and mentoring them. I'm still involved with making business decisions that support our franchisees and affect their bottom lines. I still keep my eye on the bottom line, and the Home Office focused on the things that produce growth for our franchisees.

People have asked me over the years: *How does your relationship with the Lord affect your business? What difference does being a Christian make in running your business?* Now I have an answer for them. It isn't about "seven steps to harmony in your life," or "ten principles for balancing home with business." There are thousands of variations to the challenges that hit every business, every business person, every day. No set of steps or principles could ever be comprehensive enough to help sort a path through such a jungle. But having only one primary desire in your heart is the key that opens the door to God's wisdom in every situation or circumstance. What makes a company different is determined by what is in the senior officer's heart. When God finally brings that person to a place where they care first and foremost to know Him in their life, then everything else automatically falls into place. As God instills this singular desire within your heart, it will become the passion that energizes and moves everything.

If this is already your life experience, you know what I'm talking about. If you have not yet been drawn by God into this deeper relationship with Him, this does not make you "less" of a Christian. You are exactly in the place on God's path where He has positioned you for the present time, and you can be comforted that He is progressively drawing you into greater experiences of Him as He reveals

His life in you. There is nothing better (or more peaceful) than being in the exact spot that God has chosen for you. Be comforted by the fact that this isn't something that can be rushed, or comprehended, or manufactured on our own. It is nothing we have the capacity to understand short of a revelation from God in His timing. I certainly do not have the words to convince anyone of the revolutionary power for their life that is contained in this solitary desire—and I certainly can't give anyone this passion for God—only God is able to bring each of us to a place where nothing else matters but Him.

When this happens, however, you will be forever changed. You will come to work as I do now. You will have to deal with making money, and hiring people, and having to let people go, and making decisions that affect the bottom line. But what will influence all of it (and often in ways that you presently have no awareness of) is your *primary heart's desire to know only God and to be led by Him.* This becomes the air that you breathe and the prevailing force that influences all the rest. This all results from the fact that God is working in you.

Of course, this desire need not be overt, meaning you need not make any formal announcement to staff regarding it. Rather it is hidden, entirely within your heart. God knows, and He will daily answer your prayer as the Spirit of God, like a gentle wind that refreshes the tiredness of your soul and carries upon itself the fragrance of God throughout your life and business. In countless ways, God's calling you to this motivating desire will set in motion a foundational *systemic process* that you may not even recognize early on, but will eventually change the entire organization. Some things that were previously unvalued will grow keenly important, while other former priorities may dim to insignificance.

This solitary desire becomes your life (that is, God's life in you as your life) and your light (that is, God's changing how you see things), and your daily prayer (that is, *praying without ceasing* as discussed in chapter five). To be clear: I'm not talking about a prayer of dedication, or rededication every year or two for your business. I'm talking about a prayer that feels more like breathing than anything else; it's a desire on a daily basis that hungers for God and yearns for Christ to manifest His life within you in every way—continuously. I can assure you that it is a prayer that God *will* answer *by manifesting more of Himself in your life*; and He will do so far and above your wildest expectations *(Ephesians 3:20)*. He *always* fulfills the prayer that He has placed in our hearts to pray.

Praise God, we could never do this on our own!

God instills a passion for His word and prayer.

Recently, I got a call from someone I've known for over thirty years. We once were quite close, talking every month, but over the last five or six years we have grown distant. I attributed this to how busy he was in his business and the various traumas and trials that he has endured in recent years. Nevertheless, I always looked forward to getting together with him either in person or over the phone because we had so many shared interests.

But here he was on the phone after so many years of silence.

He said, "Daryl, I've been to hell and back as you know [he had cheated on his wife with a co-worker and it nearly destroyed his marriage] but I'm at the point where I want to eat, sleep, and breathe God. I've watched what has happened to you over these years and I want to know God in the same way. I'm not talking about this in a religious way, but in a way that grips my life, where I feel God's active leading within me. I'm calling because I want to know how to hear Him talk to me. I want to hear Him talk to me daily."

I said, "Well, I'm almost hesitant to give you my answer because you've heard it all your life, just as I heard it all my life but always dismissed it.

"The answer to your question is found in the power of *God's word* and in *prayer.* That's what has profoundly affected my life over these last decades of Christian life. As I study the word a little more each year, I can feel it renewing my mind *(Romans 12:2)* and transforming my life into the truth of what I am studying. For example, I recently spent time studying the book of Ephesians where Paul speaks of *one* body, *one* God, *one* Spirit, and so forth, to stress the *unity* of believers. While studying this book, God relentlessly revealed to me the stark contrast between the truth in His word and my own life, which in hindsight I see only division with other believers. I was divided from them because of a different denominational affiliation, or a different doctrinal belief, or failures I observed in their lives that I judged to be greater than my own. Divisiveness was the hallmark of my relationships with many other believers, even with my dad.

"But today, I feel united. Why? Not because I decided one day to be different. I enjoyed 'contending' with other Christians and I earnestly thought this is what I was supposed to do. No, I'm different today because *God's word* has instilled within me a love for, and unity with, *all* believers (not in all beliefs, but in *one* Spirit). That's what God's word has the power to do. It works in your life and steadily renews your mind and transforms your living to what it says.

"God's word speaks with power and authority. God Himself said that His word is living and active, and sharper than any two-edged sword *(Hebrews 4:12)*. That is referring to how His word has the power to cut its way through all of our fleshly attitudes, concepts, and presuppositions and begin to transform our lives according to what it says. There is power in God's word to do that. So, if God has really brought you to a place where you want to live daily knowing more of Him, then He is also going to make a path for you. He might bring a friend over to invite you to a Bible study with him, or lead you to listen to a Bible study over the internet, or join a Bible study in your neighborhood or at your church fellowship. He will lead you in a way that keeps you focused on His word. In my case, the Lord used that desire to know Him by leading me to teach a Thursday night Bible study in my community. I study, in a sense, to understand a book so I am able to share it with others, but I feel its effect in my life throughout the week. That's what changed my life."

This first conversation didn't last long because I had another scheduled appointment, but it was a delight for my heart because I could see the Lord's working in this man. We agreed to talk again in a few weeks to continue our conversation. I am confident that the Lord is drawing this man to Himself in ways that are beyond my friend's wildest expectations.

When knowing the Lord is your heartbeat—as distinguished from being your religion—when knowing the Lord becomes the air that you breathe, your deepest longing, your greatest passion, then your heart's greatest inner search becomes to know the Lord in even deeper ways. In addition to God's word, two-way communion with the Lord through His Spirit within you (like the *praying without ceasing* discussion we had in chapter five) becomes an equal priority, or an equal attraction. You no longer struggle to "find time" to read God's word or to pray. When your heart's greatest passion is to know God, you have a synergistic attraction to both His word and to fellowship with His Spirit within you.

God transforms our worldly passions into a singular passion for Him.

All of this talk about the renewing power in God's living word and praying without ceasing might seem too mystical and impractical to you, but it's not. It really is quite simple and practical. Think of it this way: What is the person who has a passion for baseball attracted to? He is attracted to the things of baseball, obviously. He watches games on television or goes to see them live at the stadium. He knows the individual player and team statistics, not only for his favorite team, but other teams in the same division and across the league.

The same is true for those attracted to fishing. They are attracted to all-manner of things related to fishing: They go to their local sporting goods store to check out the new camouflaged fishing line that is so hard for fish to see in water. They listen to (and tell) their share of fishing stories, look at lures and bait, and read up on different kinds of fish, including where and how to catch them. They invest in good equipment (poles, reels, fly-tying equipment, Polaroid sunglasses, and maybe a boat), the right clothing (waders and fishing vests), and maybe even some high-tech sonar equipment, which they use to assist their own knowledge of water depths. I could go on and on with this example, but I think you get the point. For these folks, this is not work or something unpleasant; it's fun for them. They don't need to be forced into doing these things; because it comes naturally, as an outflow of their passion. *They become what they are passionate about.*

This is where things get really interesting and exciting for the business person. Unlike the baseball and fishing examples above, when God instills within you an underlying passion to know Him, this never distracts from the truly successful ways of running a business. In my experience, it is just the opposite. Those things that you are responsible for in business come into sharper focus because He begins to instill within you His ways of running a business. Things that once obsessed you, like profit and loss statements or the balance sheet, no longer hold mastery, but are transformed by God to serve you as tools for your business. If God has called you to be in business, then He will use that very business as one of the vehicles for granting your desire to know only Him.

The all-consuming passion I once had for making money has been transformed into an equally intense passion for deeply knowing God. And to be clear, I could never have accomplished even a small speck of this transformation on my own. In fact, I would *never have wanted* to do so in the first place. The thought would have been abhorrent and fearful to me. In those days, I only wanted enough God to get me into heaven when I die, not so much that it would ruin what pleasures I had in life. But God knew this; that's why He did (and continues to do) *all* of the transforming work Himself. He didn't wait for me to cooperate or partner with Him. He took my passion for making money, which enslaved me to worldly desires that resulted in all-manner of stress and anxiety in my life, and slowly converted that self-directed passion into a God-directed passion for knowing Him alone, which made me a *slave to righteousness* that continues even to this day to produce abundant joy and peace in my life.

Paul describes God's transforming work in Romans 6:17–18:

> But thanks be to God that though you were *slaves of sin,* you became *obedient from the heart* to that form of teaching to which you were committed, and having been freed from sin, you became *slaves of righteousness.*

The Greek word δουλοσ (*doulos*) is the word used for "slaves" in the verses above. *Doulos* means "one whose will is swallowed up in the will of another." Paul is saying that our will (with all of its choices and desires) was once totally swallowed up (which means: completely submerged) in Satan's will, but is now completely submerged in God's will. And greater is He who is in us than he who is in the world *(1 John 4:4).*

God has swallowed us in His will through His indwelling Son. That we now desire God-things is a testimony to the presence and power that is working in us continually. It is evidence of our eternal life, and the certainty that Christ is in us. As it is written: "For it is God who is at work in you, both to will and to work for His good pleasure" (*Philippians 2:13*).

Now when I'm asked, "How can you not be driven by the bottom line, and yet still be successful?" I respond with my own question: "Which bottom line are you talking about?" When you are driven by the *bottom line of knowing God*, He instills within you the wisdom to manage the profit and loss, and balance sheet, in balance with everything else that He is doing in your life. Your desire to know Him is not stored away in some footlocker on your way home from work. You carry that desire home with you, and He begins to affect your family life as well as your business.

His wisdom, which is different than the earthly wisdom for doing just about anything, will affect you as the husband that God desires for you to be to your wife, and the father God desires you to be to your kids, and yes, even in running a business with compassion for the people who work with you. He gives you the wisdom to bring all of this into harmony and balance. There are lots of self-help books out there on this very topic, but in my experience, the one sure way to bring a peaceful balance and harmony into your life, without even being aware of it, is a *passion to know God*. This, of course, is nothing you can pump up in yourself, but it is a gift freely given by Him (*James 1:5*).

As you desire only Him, He will either make you a good steward in business or He will lead you out of business for yourself and into the employ of someone else. If He keeps you in business, then He will draw you to honor your financial commitments. He will touch your heart to keep your word with vendors, to pay them on time. He will give you the desire to treat all employees honorably and respectfully. You will grow to see the critical difference, at an experiential level, between a diligent attention to the bottom line (and realizing how important it is) versus being controlled and driven by the bottom line.

The more that God reveals Himself to us, in all His awesome sovereignty and glory, in His covenantal promises and in the redemptive mission of His Son and the faithful guidance and protection of His nurturing Spirit, the more our passion to know Him grows. What God has done in this process is place us on His ever-brightening path of righteousness *(Proverbs 4:18)* where He is bringing us to trust Him for everything *(Proverbs 3:5–6)*. The more we see God, the brighter this path becomes, and the more humbling it is. And this grows our increasingly humble desire to see more and experience more of Him. That is the effect of it. He is so magnetically attractive.

I used to think that I had to have a ministry; I have to be witnessing; I have to be able to check off of my "to-do" list what I did each day for God. But today, I just go through life. And the people that God purposes to influence through me (or for me to be influenced by) appear for a reason. *I'm simply living my life.* I'm getting up in the morning, running my four miles, hugging my wife, going to work, having a passion to know God.

That's it, that's all, there's nothing else added. God's "X" factor in running a business is a gift from Him: a *passion* for knowing Him alone!

Chapter Eight:

A Simplified Life

(God aligns our workplace with His workplace)

"The unfolding of Your words gives light;
it gives understanding to the simple."

PSALM 119:130

There are very few people these days who consider a "simplified life" to be attainable in any form. Most think that life is complex, complicated, and getting harder to cope with all the time. Both secular and Christian bookstores are filled with self-help books to aid in balancing, prioritizing, organizing, or otherwise managing this complexity (and the stress and hardships associated with it). Yet scripture assures us of something entirely different. That God's ways are not our ways and His thoughts are not our thoughts *(Isaiah 55:8)*. That the Christian life is "light," "easy," "restful," *(Matthew 11:29–30)*, "peaceful" *(Hebrews 12:11)*, "not burdensome" *(1 John 5:3–4)*, full of "freedom" *(Galatians 5:1)*, and yes, even "simple" *(2 Corinthians 11:3)*.

Let's explore more deeply what this *simplified life* looks like in practical terms.

The focus of the last chapter revealed how God instills a passion within us to truly know Him: to bring us to a place where our primary heart's desire is to genuinely be led by God and to trust Him for everything. Is this something we can speed along through our own effort to help God? No, this is done entirely within *God's workplace,* solely by God's working within our hearts and minds, and according to His timing and wisdom over the course of our lives. However, as God instills this primary desire within us, our own earthly passions and priorities in life naturally begin to evolve. We likely will not be aware of this transformational change at first. Yet, as God works continuously to renew and transform our hearts and minds, our awareness of things around us grows more sensitive to God's speaking and leading, and our thinking is increasingly renewed and transformed, leading to a progressively simplified life. Our lives become simpler because our motivations become purer as a result of God's workings.

God's plan for us is really simple.

The good news about all of this is the fact that God is mindful that we are but dust *(Psalm 103:14),* so His plan for us is *really* simple. Consider Ephesians 2:1 for a moment and you will know what I mean. While we were yet *dead* in our trespasses and sins—meaning, at a time when we could do absolutely nothing for ourselves—God was already working for our benefit by paving the way for our simplified lives in Him.

On our own, prior to Christ's life being revealed in us, all we managed to do was wallow in sin, but God sent

His Son, who gave Himself for our sins so that He might rescue us from this present evil age *(Galatians 1:4)* and give us eternal life *(John 3:16)*. He sealed us with the Holy Spirit of promise *(Ephesians 1:13)* and came to dwell in us as our hope of glory *(Colossians 1:27)*. He became to us *wisdom* from God, and our righteousness, sanctification, and redemption *(1 Corinthians 1:30)*. In other words, He became everything we need both in this life and throughout eternity.

Then to make this abundantly clear, Christ communicated this eternal truth to us in the form of an analogy—a simple word picture that described us as His sheep and He as our shepherd *(John 10:7–11, 26–30)*. I don't believe Christ's reference to sheep, here, was arbitrary or some sort of capricious accident. Of all the animals He could have chosen, He picked sheep to most accurately represent those whom the Father sent Him to care for, and to do so in the role of a shepherd caring for His flock.

If you've had the chance to observe domesticated herd animals, you know that sheep (both individually and collectively) are about as dumb and helpless an animal as they come. Perhaps a kinder way of saying this is that they are "simple" minded. If they are to be kept safe and healthy, they need to be led everywhere by their shepherd: to water, to grazing land for food, and to a protected enclave at night. Without a shepherd, most sheep wouldn't have the sense to come out of the rain, find food and water, or avoid falling into the nearest ditch and breaking a leg. That's the animal Christ chose to describe us. Does that paint a clear enough picture for why we need things to be simple?

It's like Christ saying to us: "Listen, I'm going to rescue you from the eternally destructive mess you've gotten yourselves in, and I'm going to put myself in you, and I'm going to increasingly draw you to talk to Me, and listen to Me, and I'm going to *make you know* everything you need to know when you need to know it. I'm going to do all of this because you can't do it yourself. So, I'll be your Shepherd, just as you are the sheep that your heavenly Father has given Me to care for."

Now, thirty years ago, I would have acknowledged intellectually that all of the verses listed above did, in fact, say exactly what I just represented them to say. However, at that stage in my life, these verses would not have penetrated my heart and mind to the point where my life was naturally changed because of it. Today, however, I can look back over those decades and recognize that all of these verses are continuing to become progressively true in my experience.

God simplifies our lives by giving us His wisdom for every situation.

By now, I think you understand why I titled this book *The Simplified Life*. It is the title that best describes the overall trajectory of my life over these last fifty years in business. From a life of frenetic complexity, anxiety, and stress, to a simplified life of peace and rest, guided daily by God's wisdom in ways that I never thought possible even thirty years ago. When you have only one primary desire in your heart—to genuinely know God—this *really* simplifies things.

Remember the example of Solomon from chapter five? God promised to give Solomon His wisdom, and scripture records the fact that He never failed in delivering that wisdom, precisely when Solomon needed it and in the form most beneficial to his circumstances. Can you imagine how much simpler Solomon's life was after receiving such a promise from God? Why would Solomon worry and fret over problems he faced? He knew that God would provide the wisdom he needed, when and in the form he needed it. This solitary promise from God would take *all* the stress out of living life, wouldn't it?

Well, here is some really good news. God has made this very same promise to us today! The Creator God's wisdom now dwells *in us* and is available to us in every situation we face. This is not some esoteric or theoretical doctrine to be conceptualized only intellectually. His wisdom is available for us to *experience* in practical terms and *at a level of detail* that results in a life that is truly simple and uncomplicated. If you still doubt this, reread First Corinthians 1:30 again. Christ has been made to us "wisdom from God."

With God's wisdom dwelling *in us*, we need not "try" to figure out His leading, or to harmonize conflicting interests swirling around a chaotic situation, or to live a "balanced" life. All such considerations go out the window when we simply live our lives with an abiding desire to know only Him. God is faithful to provide His wisdom to us in every situation, when we need it and in the form most beneficial for our good. It may come in the form of a spontaneous thought, or a word from scripture, or an answer to prayer, or a comment from a loved one or friend. God *will* bring His wisdom to you. You can live your life without fear, stress, or worry, knowing that you haven't "missed" something you need to do or understand. If you need to know something or be directed in some way, *God will make you know* His direction for you. If He is silent, it's not because He is mad at you. It means He is handling the situation on your behalf at the moment, in his timing, and without the need for any action on your part. This is God's simple approach to life: He does it all, and He is all we need. As He draws us to focus on Him, He directs our paths. As we plan our way through life, He directs our steps *(Proverbs 16:9)*.

Our flesh, of course, always stirs itself up to oppose or distract us from activities like relaxing in the Lord, reading our Bible, praying, or patiently trusting that if God wills for us to do or see something He will put it right in front of us. But this is precisely the *simplified life,* full of peace and rest, that God calls us to enjoy today. I don't have to go crazy trying to figure out God's will or His wisdom for a particular problem. Christ in us is God's wisdom for *every* situation we face. We can *never* find the kind of wisdom that makes life simple apart from Him.

God simplifies our lives by altering our hearts and minds.
I readily acknowledge that *how* the Lord does this transformational work in us is beyond our comprehension. It defies our earthly human logic. It isn't something that we are consciously aware of as it happens. Of course, since this is entirely God's work and not our own, we really don't need to understand how *God is God* in such matters, or how He speaks forth His new creation in our lives, out of nothing, just as He did in His original creation. What we can acknowledge, however, is God's work in us from the fact that we somehow believe in God and are drawn to think of Him and trust Him. This is not the natural state of humanity. Absent God's Spirit dwelling in us by faith, we would have no interest in God at all *(Romans 1:29–32)*.

In our human thinking, all of life's decisions *must* be reconciled within our own reason and logic. Add to this our conflicting emotions, and those around us, and the world of decision-making becomes a brutal maze of complexity and confusion before we know it. But God's way of decision-making is truly easy. He will make you to know what you need to know...when you need to know it.

I started business consumed with this human thinking, filled with a bitter brew of fear, pride, anxiety, and stress about *every* decision I made. Even fifty years ago, the speed in which an unhappy customer was willing to drop their commercial building service contract was breathtaking—and rightfully so in many cases. If they arrived to a poorly cleaned office, with no paper towels in the bathrooms or trash left in wastebaskets, they had every right to expect that we would arrive as soon as possible to rectify the problem. These were legitimately *urgent* situations, where we had to marshal our forces and immediately respond to that customer's needs. If we failed to do so, our company's services could be terminated. These were not problems you could pray about for three days before taking action.

But because of my own pride and fear of failure, I was incapable of objectively differentiating an *urgent* situation from one that was *not urgent*. My pride insisted on making *everything* a crisis, to soothe my fear of failing, which was really just another propped-up idol from my flesh.

If I didn't solve every problem immediately, within hours on the same day it arose, then such a delay (in my mind) would surely lead (in a matter of days) to the loss of the entire business. To my thinking, the company was perpetually on the brink of collapse. This ever-escalating level of stress drove sleep from my body and eventually drove me to seek medical help, which in turn, led me into the sedating world of prescription drugs. The *human answer* to all of this consuming stress played out on this formula: more stress equals more daily Valium consumption! I eventually got to the point where I was losing a grip on reality altogether.

This was the pitiful state of my life when I stood by my Cousin Dave's bed staring at the tangible peace radiating from him. I see now how God brought me to that place in my life where I was broken to the point that all the money and temporal achievements in my life seemed meaningless. All I wanted was to know God, and I silently cried out to Him from my heart that simple prayer.

I see today that He has been answering that prayer (a prayer that He caused me to pray) ever since. Gradually, over the course of many years, He has been faithful to bring me into a closer relationship with Him, which in turn, has radically altered *what* I feel and *how* I think about situations and circumstances around me. But this didn't happen all at once; rather, it was a gradual process. Over those same years I would argue vociferously with myself, back and forth, something like this:

> *I've GOT to take care of this problem—or lose my business!*
> **Pray. God will make me to know how to deal with the problem.**
> *No! I haven't heard from Him for 5 days! I've got to act.*
> **Keep praying—and until God brings an action to mind, He's handling it.**

I don't know that! Maybe I haven't heard from Him for a month! I'm not sure who or what I'm listening to any-more—is it Him or not? When I pray to Him, I don't hear anything any way.

Then there's nothing to know or He would have told you. Just rest in the Promised Land—rest in His arms.

Thank God He made things simple! All the while I was arguing with myself, He was still my faithful Shepherd. I was oblivious to the changes He was working in my heart and mind to trust Him more. My focus was often entirely on the problems before me in *my workplace*. But His focus and activity was on *His workplace in my heart and mind*. At this point in my life, and for years following, I felt (like maybe ninety-nine percent of the time) that I didn't know how to listen to God at all, let alone have confidence that it was Him I was listening to. But my Great Shepherd knew that. He kept it simple and guided me along His path. The frustration I was experiencing, as reflected in the in-ternal heated conversation I just cited, was sourced in my continual effort to *do* something, *anything*, as if it was *my* re-sponsibility to "hear" God when He spoke. If I didn't hear Him immediately, then something was wrong. I was still struggling to "be led by Him," which really meant that I was still trying to be the shepherd, rather than rest in the fact that I was only a sheep. How dumb was that? I have the How-Great-Thou-Art Almighty God committed to me as my Shepherd, yet I still insist on trying to lead?

Stop a moment and think about this last point: Is there anything that He, God our Shepherd, wouldn't do for His sheep? He gave His own life for the sheep that His Father placed in His care. Every Christian is part of that flock of sheep. So in the midst of my problems, precisely when I need Him most, is He going to say, "Um, sorry, but it's now your turn. You have to figure this mess out for yourself. Good luck with that! Too bad you're just a dumb sheep because you could really use a little wisdom right now." Is He going to walk off and leave me stranded to fend for myself? What good shepherd would do such a thing?

This process over our lifetime, while it appears mysterious to our eyes and thinking, is really Christ spreading His life in and through us as He promised He would do. I understood this transforming work of Christ, as a doctrine intellectually, from a very early age in my Christian walk, but now I have tasted the power of His divine life within me changing the very way I think and trust Him for things. Consider this absolute truth: that the God of creation—who simply spoke forth His word—and all of creation sprang forth *out of nothing* in obedience to Him. That powerful Creator God is the very person who is *now living in us*; and He is *still* a speaking God! He delights in sharing Himself (and His wisdom) with us. Who calls into being that which does not exist *(Romans 4:17)*, and who has chosen to reveal Himself to us through His spoken word. He is still writing on the tablets of our hearts today *(2 Corinthians 3:3)*.

From my experience, I had nothing to do with any of this (and I *still* don't). Such transformative work can only be wrought by God's divine life coming into my dead carcass, this human life of mine, and bringing forth His eternal life within me. From my perspective, He has a long way to go with me yet, but I must acknowledge to God's glory alone that He has literally created a new me within me. Christ has been faithfully transforming me by the renewing of my mind *(Romans 12:2; Ephesians 4:23)* and transforming me into His image, from glory to glory, just as from the Lord, the Spirit *(2 Corinthians 3:18)*. We truly have peace with God through our Lord Jesus Christ *(Romans 5:1)*. And over the course of our lives, God draws us to set "aside the old self with its evil purposes," and put on the "new self who is being renewed to a true knowledge according to the image of the One who created" us *(Colossians 3:9–10)*. This divine process takes time. It's not like a light switch that can be flipped on. It's not something you can grasp with the intellect. It results from Christ's renewing work in our hearts, continually bringing us deeper into the true knowledge of Him. As 2 Peter 1:2–3 declares:

> Grace and peace be multiplied to you in the knowledge of God and of Jesus our Lord; seeing that His divine power has granted to us *everything pertaining to life* and godliness, *through the true knowledge of Him* who called us by His own glory and excellence.

Again I say, how He grows this passion for knowing Him alters our hearts and minds in the process, and progressively grows His life in us, is impossible to fully comprehend with our human mind. The only thing you realize over time is that you see things differently today than you did five years ago, or ten years ago. You think differently than you did five years ago, or ten years ago. This is added proof that He has renewed your mind and transformed you from glory to glory a bit more each passing year. It is amazing. It is not something you achieve, and then move on from. It is a progressive thing that grows God's glorious enlightenment within you every day of your life. We will never be free of our flesh, of course, or be fully transformed until the Lord's return, but the joy and peace that Christ brings to us along the way, as our Great Shepherd, is beyond description. It truly is a simplified life.

God simplifies our lives by healing our eyes and ears.
An associate and I had a good laugh over the antics of his five-year-old grandson. We were really laughing at ourselves because the actions of this child are so reflective of what we do as adults. Apparently, this young boy loves to "read" books. At this point in his young life, he is beginning to learn his alphabet and how to phonetically sound out each letter of a word to understand its meaning. But when he was three, he was convinced beyond doubt that he *already knew* how to read. He didn't, of course, but that didn't stop him from believing it and refusing any assistance to the contrary. One day, after his parents had been reading his picture books to him for some time (the kind of book with big bright pictures of trucks or animals and seven to ten words per page) he announced that *he* would do *all* the "reading" of his books to his parents from now on.

He then proceeded to "read" his favorite books with great efficiency. To the casual observer, it certainly did look like this three-year-old had already learned to read. But wait a minute, not so fast. When asked to read the sign on a truck or building within a picture, something that was not normally read by his parents, he was stumped. To divert attention from this obvious embarrassment, he would get huffy and demand that others be quiet while he was reading. In truth, he wasn't reading at all, but only repeating what he had committed to memory. He saw the words and was convinced that he knew how to read them, but the words at that point in his young life had no real meaning at all. Eventually, however, as he learns his alphabet in school, then the phonetics these letters make within a word and sentence, he will gain a true knowledge of reading that will eventually lead him to experience the joy of reading books first hand, not simply as a parrot mimicking what someone else has said.

I share this story as an example for why understanding something doctrinally is usually not enough. As a preacher's kid, I picked up the so-called meaning of hundreds of scripture verses, based on what others had told me the verse said (and meant), without taking the time to prayerfully seek out the Lord's wisdom to instruct me personally regarding the meaning of the verse. Extend that same lazy habit to situations involving our daily living. Rarely do we begin with God's wisdom—His thoughts, ways, and understandings—regarding a matter before us. We don't have the eyes to see the situation as He sees it, or the ears to hear the things important to Him. Yes, we have possession of our own earthly life experiences (which in my case were mostly self-centered) and our own thoughts and insights, but this entire collection may be little more than childish earthly wisdom compared to the rich storehouse of heavenly wisdom that God has made available to us in Christ.

Let me put some words down on paper and let you read them. Then we will look to the Lord to guide us concerning how much, or little, we actually understand of what we have read when guided only by our own experience. I could say to you the following and it would all be accurate, yet the words may still tell you little or nothing. I could say to you:

> As you desire only Him, He will either make you a good steward in business or He will lead you out of business for yourself and into the employ of someone else. If He keeps you in business, then He will draw you to honor your financial commitments. He will touch your heart to keep your word with vendors, to pay them on time. He will give you the desire to treat all employees honorably and respectfully. And He will cause you to be diligent and truthful to your customers regardless of the consequences. You will grow to see the critical difference, at an experiential level, between a diligent attention to the bottom line (and realizing the importance of it) versus being controlled and driven by the bottom line.

Had I read this short paragraph thirty years ago, I would have concluded: *Okay, I need to pay my vendors on time, treat my employees fairly, and be truthful to my customers.* And all of that would be true, but this is far short of the heavenly wisdom that God will grow in us over time. In our own eyes, we may view ourselves as honoring our financial commitments, or one who is fair and honest, but we may not be. We lack the kind of wisdom and insight needed to see ourselves in true light, based solely on our earthly wisdom at the time. All of us suffer from this. Our flesh is a repository of all-manner of self-delusion. The good news is that we don't have to struggle to figure this out; God will make us aware of any areas in our life where we are living according to our own wisdom rather than His divine wisdom—the wisdom that leads to true success and a simplified life.

Regarding employees, for example, He takes us beyond a policy that imposes "fairness" in the workplace, to a place where He opens our eyes to see things we never saw before, and our hearing to hear things we never heard before. He makes us sensitive to more than merely the spoken word being uttered, but tunes our sensitivities to pick up nuances of body language and subtle inflections of speech. He brings us beyond only *hearing* what is being said, to actually *listening and understanding* what is being communicated, including the implications of its meaning for the employee. In all of our relationships with employees, He changes our hearts to show us what He wants us to know about them. He will give us compassion for them as people, as equal creations of God, and for their needs beyond the business paycheck. He will make us sensitive to the fact that many employees have devastatingly difficult backgrounds. They may have no peace anywhere else in their lives, and they are just trying to keep it together from day to day.

As you desire to know God, will God lead you to be fair with your employees? Yes, of course He will, but it's far more than that. He gives you a sensitivity you never had before. He gives you His wisdom regarding the needs of a particular person who works with you. And you may be the only one in that person's life that has the hope of God the Creator in them. God has brought them into your life, not just for a paycheck, but because He has placed them in your care as a representative steward of God in their lives. He makes you aware of that, as an outflow of your passion to know Him—a passion that He has instilled within your heart. You don't have to try to educate yourself, or set up some campaign to gather this data. What I am talking about is so elusive that it will easily slip through any program you contrive to discover it. But God will reveal it to you in His timing, and bring you to understand all of what He intends for you to know. As He focuses you on a passion to know Him, He is going to reveal His desire (and the things He wants you to know) concerning the employees He has placed in your care. He will do so again and again in many situations, and in miraculous ways, to the point where they see the hope of Him, the light of Him, and the peace of Him in your life and in your dealings with them. Not through a religious tract that you slip into their paycheck, but in what they feel from your heart during their interactions with you, and in what they see in your actions and treatment of them.

Regarding vendors, it's not just a matter of paying them on time. God will make you realize that vendors are more than the lowest bidder in a competitive process. They are people too, and an equal creation of God. As God gives you His wisdom, you begin to see what you never saw before—that this vendor just had his spouse leave him, or had a family member die, or was diagnosed with cancer, or just found out that his kid is addicted to drugs. Perhaps he is hanging on by a thread financially even though he is trying to keep a smile on his face for you because he doesn't want you to be disappointed in him. God begins to give you wisdom beyond the handshake and the façade smile;

He does so because as much as He is working in our lives, He is also working *through our lives* for the benefit of those people that he brings into contact with us.

Regarding customers, it is more than being honest with them. God surely does free us, and instills within us a pure desire to deal with all of our customers honestly and forthrightly. But we also realize that the opportunity to serve a particular customer didn't just happen. It has a greater purpose than just cleaning and polishing floors, even though we don't always know what that is at the time. This understanding, during whatever time we are allowed to service them, gives us the freedom to deal honestly with them in all things, to never oversell or misrepresent ourselves, and to own up to our failures without obfuscation, regardless of the consequences. In the end, God heals our sight to see that customers are people too—people that God has placed in our lives for a purpose.

God simplifies our lives by aligning our workplace with His workplace.
Our corporate tag line, "It's about Lives," is a perfect example of what I am talking about regarding employees, vendors, and customers. For the first twenty-five years in business, Environment Control's corporate motto was "Taking an ordinary job and accomplishing something with it." I am praying as I write this because what I am sharing with you now reflects the essence of this chapter, and possibly the entire book.

One day, I went into a meeting with my top staff and said, "I need to tell you something that I've been feeling for some time now. I just don't feel comfortable with our corporate motto anymore. I haven't figured it out totally, but I wanted you all to know that I'm uncomfortable with it."

One staffer asked, "Why aren't you comfortable with it?"

I said, "I don't really know for sure, but I see our business, and those of us who work in this business, as being involved in something much deeper than what this old motto reflects. We're not primarily about getting an account, cleaning toilets, making a profit, and building a business. We're about something more than that...somehow. That's all I know right now."

I asked all of them to think and pray about it. Over the course of the following year, we revisited this topic and had numerous discussions about the pros and cons of various new corporate mottos, but none really stuck. Then one day, some of us were in the parking lot helping a new owner pick up his initial equipment and supplies. He was leaving directly from our office to drive to his franchise location and begin his new franchise business. It was an exciting milestone for him and us.

As this man drove off, one of my staff said, "Boy, I really care about that guy."

That simple comment struck me like a lightning bolt. I thought, *That's it! That's what we're all about. What we do here is about people's lives.* It wasn't long before one of the staff, I don't remember who, coined the phrase that governs our company to this day: *"It's About Lives."*

That is what the wisdom of God brings to you. I shared with you in chapter one that I believed people—employees, vendors, and customers—were the source of all my problems. But God had now brought me to a place where I considered these very same people to be the sole reason

why I was in business at all. They were no longer problems, but blessings to me. Only God could accomplish such
a transformation in my heart toward the people He was
bringing into my life on a daily basis. God also made these
men and women in His own image. He knows the number
of hairs on every head. He knows the pain, the hardship,
the stress in the lives of every person we meet and what He
has planned for them. As He aligns *our workplace* with *His
workplace,* the love in His heart for these people becomes
our own heartbeat, as our passion for Him grows.

The Lord gives us the wisdom we need: to be truly successful in the business He has called us to work in as *our
workplace,* and to produce the peace that He grows in us
as part of *His workplace.* He is the good Shepherd over our
lives, and He brings *our workplace* in alignment with *His
workplace* through the course of our lives, often in ways that
we could never anticipate or dream of. While we were operating with our workplace motto—"taking an ordinary job
and accomplishing something with it"—God's workplace
motto was "taking some ordinary sheep and accomplishing something with them." Eventually, all of our individual
mottos and motivations drop away, and we are left with
God's passion within:

It's About Lives.

That is the good news gospel of God in each of our lives.
Let's close this book with a prayer from the Apostle Paul
that is as relevant today (and to our discussion) as it was
when he first uttered it to, and on behalf of, the Ephesians:

When I think of the wisdom and scope of his plan
I fall down on my knees and pray to the Father of
all the great family of God...that out of his glorious, unlimited resources he will give you the
mighty inner strengthening of his Holy Spirit. And
I pray that Christ will be more and more at home
in your hearts, living within you as you trust in
him. May your roots go down deep into the soil of
God's marvelous love; and may you be able to feel
and understand, as all God's children should, how
long, how wide, how deep, and how high his love
really is; and to experience this love for yourselves,
though it is so great that you will never see the end
of it or fully know or understand it. And so at last
you will be filled up with God himself. Now glory
be to God who by his mighty power at work within
us is able to do far more than we would ever dare to
ask or even dream of—infinitely beyond our high-
est prayers, desires, thoughts, or hopes. May he be
given glory forever and ever through endless ages...
through Jesus Christ."

EPHESIANS 3:14–21, TLB

Amen.

Addendum:

A Simplified Life Potpourri

(*A Hotchpot of experience from 50 years of business*)

Not that we are adequate in ourselves to consider anything as coming from ourselves, but our adequacy is from God.

2 CORINTHIANS 3:5

As you can imagine, attempting to chronicle fifty years of experience is an impossible task for one book. My initial notes for this project would fill three volumes of twice the thickness as the single volume you are now holding in your hand. This led me to prayerfully scrutinize and prioritize what I considered to be God's essential truths for everyone, whether they are in business, employed or unemployed, in Christian ministry, or in whatever situation they found themselves at the point when God brings this book across their path. I have placed these essential truths in the first eight chapters.

However, this leaves reams of additional experiences, which certain individuals may benefit from. Thus, I have included some of this here in a potpourri format:

1. "Cloaked in Righteousness"

My soul will exult in my God;
For he has clothed me with garments of salvation,
He has wrapped me with a robe of righteousness.
ISAIAH 61:10

I was taken by surprise when God first brought this familiar verse from Isaiah to life in my heart. I had never really thought of salvation in terms of a robe before. I thought of it more like a "ticket"—one that ultimately got me into heaven. This left me continually troubled with how God sees me *in this life*. But scripture tells us that our salvation is a robe of righteousness that God sees us completely wrapped in as we go through *this life* and for eternity.

2. "Freedom from Self-Effort"

All our righteous deeds are like a filthy garment.
ISAIAH 64:6

Somehow, the familiarity of this verse allowed me, for decades, to gloss over its true meaning. Every time I encountered the words *filthy garment*, or as the King James puts it, *filthy rags*, I thought it referred to the evil we do. But notice, the prophet isn't describing our *evil* deeds here; he's talking about our *good* ones! To a holy, just, and righteous

God, even the "best" things we do are filthy rags. Our only boast is in *Christ Jesus,* our total righteousness! This means that *He* is our total and sole goodness! I am often asked whether I am implying that we should stop giving to our churches or to the poor, or other kinds of things normally associated with the Christian life. My answer is, "Not at all." The Bible clearly enjoins us to love our neighbor, help the poor, support our church, and so forth. What this verse tells me is that unless it is Christ Himself inspiring and carrying out those works *through* us, they have no real value. If we are doing them out of guilt, fear, or obligation they are for not.

3. "Freedom from Inadequacy"

Not that we are adequate in ourselves to consider any-thing as coming from ourselves, but our adequacy is from God.

2 CORINTHIANS 3:5

Adequate? The same word John the Baptist used when he declared, concerning Christ, "I am not *fit* to remove His sandals" *(Matthew 3:11)* and which the centurion used when he said to Jesus, "Lord, I am not *worthy* for You to come under my roof" *(Matthew 8:8).* It is a word encompassing both the *measure* and *quality* of one's sufficiency, the extent to which we are considered *good enough.* Somehow, that deeply felt necessity had gotten all mixed up in my mind with the belief that it was up to me to "do" something or "be" someone. My presupposition was that my self-worth depended on *my* ability to please other people and God. By contrast, Paul declares that the true source of all adequacy lies *outside* of us. It isn't dependent on the "effectiveness" of our lives. It isn't the result of controlling our own circumstances or gaining the respect of other people. Rather, the basis of our self-worth—and by extension, of any genuine peace and contentment—rests entirely in one objective, reliable, and unchanging reality: *the sufficiency and perfection of God Himself.*

4. "Contentment in Everything"

> *I have learned to be content in whatever circumstances I am [in].*
> PHILIPPIANS 4:11

I was amazed when I first saw this verse. *Content?* What does that mean? How could anyone, even the Apostle Paul, be content in difficult situations? After all, any contentment I had ever experienced was largely a function of believing that I was in a position of control, in a position to arrange all the cards in my life: career, health, finances, reputation, kids, spouse, you name it. But clearly, Paul was not referring to that. Hadn't he penned those words from prison, while accused on false pretenses, stripped of all ability to control his own destiny, and completely dependent on the gifts of others? His contentment did not arise from favorable circumstances, or other people's actions, or his ability to control the events swirling around him. Not at all! His contentment was not based on any circumstance or situation, but on the *person* of Christ Jesus living within him and filling him with *His* contentment.

5. "Criticism is My Friend"

He whose ear listens to the life-giving reproof
Will dwell among the wise…
He who listens to reproof acquires understanding.
PROVERBS 15:31–32

While these verses in Proverbs are referring to the *life-giving* reproof that comes from scripture, God also brings His *life-giving* speaking to us in many forms: from our spouses, kids, neighbors, a perfect stranger, or a customer. When others criticize or complain, the words themselves may be spoken out of anger or frustration, and may be hurtful to hear. During the immediacy of the situation, it is difficult to interpret anything "life-giving" within those words. Yet God is at work in them. He is turning every negative word spoken and every painful situation faced into something good for us (Romans 8:28): perhaps something that turns us to Him in prayer, or something that reveals a fleshly proclivity or character weakness in our hearts. God is redeeming every negative in your life by transforming it into a positive for your good.

Growing in this understanding over many years, complaints and criticism no longer possess the destructive power they once held for me. In fact, I've actually come to view them as allies—as essential components to the success of any company. Complaints serve as powerful incentives to improve overall business excellence, whether quality of personnel, training, supervision, or motivation. They clarify precisely what customers and clients need and give us the opportunity to show, by our response, how committed we are to serving those needs. Furthermore, criticism and complaints convey a personal benefit, since how we react to them gives us insight into the state of our character. It exposes those areas in which we are continuing to rely on our flesh rather than God's sufficiency, and allows us to experience how the Lord is increasingly transforming us into His likeness.

Of course, not all criticism can be readily characterized as "life-giving;" and at times we do need to look past certain destructive elements if we are to extract any benefit. But at these times, I have found excellent advice in the words of a company vice-president and wise friend from years ago. He used to say, "Don't listen to *who* said it or *how* they said it. Just ask the Lord, '*Is there any truth in it?*'" Focusing on the "who" and the "how" turns the situation into a personal, emotionally charged contest between winners and losers where the truth can easily become obscured. The Spirit bringing to our remembrance that we are clothed in Christ's robe frees us to move beyond our negative emotions to hear valuable information we might otherwise miss. Because we understand that criticism can never detract from our worth in God's eyes, we enjoy a freedom and peace when hearing the wisdom and direction inherent in the critique of others.

6. "A Heart on its Knees"

Search me, O God, and know my heart: try me, and know my thoughts;
And see if there be any wicked way in me, and lead me in the everlasting way.

PSALM 139:23–24

Today, I want to live in the freedom and rest of God's leading. I no longer want to obsess about *how* God is going to direct me or *when* it's going to happen or *what* I need to do first. I am content to live in constant awareness that the Lord, in His sovereignty, is already arranging every detail of my life. His Spirit within will cause me, in His time, to know and act in conformity to His will. In my experience, this did not happen during those years when I was just "visiting" the Christian life, when I thought of God as another "thing" in my life that needed to be balanced along with everything else. True freedom only comes when we say, "Lord, I want to know You in place of everything else. Keep my heart on its knees before You." Only when the Lord brings us to live daily in this place, do we begin to experience the peace that passes ALL understanding.

7. "Filled with the Fullness of God"

*For this reason I kneel before the Father, from whom his whole family in heaven and on earth derives its name. I pray that out of his glorious riches he may strengthen you with power through his Spirit in your inner being, so that Christ may dwell in your hearts through faith. And I pray that you, being rooted and established in love, may have power, together with all the saints, to grasp how wide and long and high and deep is the love of Christ, and to know this love that surpasses knowledge—**that you may be filled to the measure of all the fullness of God.***
Ephesians 3:14–19 NIV

Here is an amazing reality: when we let go of the death grip we have on our own destiny, the very fulfillment of our dreams (which we always thought would come through a spouse, kids, success, dream house, ideal job, or whatever) turns out to be far greater than anything we originally conceived. Everything else pales in comparison. There comes a moment in which God reveals His life in stark relief to all that dark weight of our fleshly longing. It's as if a light goes on deep in our hearts. God's divine life becomes a magnetic, irresistible attraction, and we sense the drawing power of His life within us. We feel the scriptures come alive; we experience what we read changing our lives from the inside out. Then we begin to *know Him and the power of His resurrection (Philippians 3:10).* And even though that power is still contained in the fleshly "clay pot" of our humanity, we see it progressively conforming us to the likeness of Jesus Christ. At the same time, He is manifesting His presence to others around us, causing many people we know—and some we don't—to say, "I want to know the same God of peace, the same God of gentleness, the same God of compassion, the same God of forgiveness that [insert your name] knows."

8. "A Rest for Today"

> *Come to Me, all who are weary and heavy-laden ... and I will give you rest.*
> MATTHEW 11:28

I have known this verse since childhood, but I always assumed that the *rest* Jesus referred to related to a future time of everlasting life with Him in heaven. But this was only my presupposition of what scripture really says. I now recognize that the Lord was also offering something for the here-and-now, a *rest* that we can experience in the midst of the practical details of everyday life. Jesus was saying in essence, "Don't just wait until you get to heaven. Come to Me today with all your burdens: financial burdens, health burdens, personnel burdens, marriage burdens, parenting burdens—for in those things, I want to give you rest."

9. "Knowing God's Will"

> *At the end of three days the officers…commanded the people, saying, "**When you see** the Ark of the Covenant of the LORD your God with the Levitical priests carrying it, then you shall set out from your place and go after it. However, there shall be between you and it a distance of about 2,000 cubits by measure. Do not come near it, that you may know the way by which you shall go, for you have not passed this way before.*
>
> JOSHUA 3:2–4

Precisely when the way before us looks most precarious and uncertain, the Lord comes to us and shares three little words designed to restore our faith and transform our fears into confident trust: *When you see.* Yes, waiting can be frustrating, but God promised to show us when to move and the direction we should move. If we are not clear on God's move, we wait.

Consider the Israelites. One thing is certain. No attentive Israelite could have possibly failed to notice the brilliance of the Ark as it passed by; that small, gold chest was the visible symbol of *God's presence* among His people. Even the Ark's contents spoke of how He had led and cared for them during their long sojourn in the wilderness. First, the Ten Commandments represented all of God's words; second, Aaron's staff represented His miracle-working power; and third, the bowl of manna represented the Lord's daily provision for all their needs.

If God led the Israelites to their rest in such a clear and visible way, surely He will not play hide-and-seek with us! As an earthly father—if I could foresee every decision that would bring my kids true success, joy, peace, and fulfillment—even I would never consider being vague with them! How much more unlikely, then, that our heavenly Father would do so with His dear children?

If you then, being evil, know how to give good gifts to your children, how much more will your Father who is in heaven give what is good to those who ask Him (Matthew 7:11)!

10. "God's Promise of Discernment"

You will discern righteousness and justice and equity and every good course.
PROVERBS 2:9

This was a verse God led me to immediately after my experience with Him at the side of Dave's hospital bed. At the time, I remember being touched by God regarding the word *discern*. I recognized then that this word inherently refers to something that was possible for me to experience. Now, I am impressed with a different word in this same verse. The word *every* also confirms that God is also minding each particular detail of my life. He *promises* to cause us to discern *every good course* in our lives. Not some, not most, but *every* good course!

11. "The Power of God's Word"

> *This book of the law shall not depart from your mouth, but you shall meditate on it day and night, so that you may be careful to do according to all that is written in it; for then you will make your way prosperous, and then you will have success.*
> JOSHUA 1:8

Joshua was facing the prospect of unrelenting warfare with enemies far greater in number and weaponry than those of the Israelites. Before him lay a minefield of difficult decisions and challenges. Can you identify with Joshua's plight? Sounds like living in modern times, doesn't it? But instead of offering military intelligence or some sure-fire, ten-step strategy for conquering the land of Canaan, God told Joshua to simply keep his focus—24/7—on the scriptures as the one prescription guaranteed to bring victory in any and all situations.

Be anxious for nothing (Philippians 4:6).

He is mindful that we are but dust (Psalm 103:14).

In the day you cried out I answered you (Psalm 138:3).

Cast all your care upon Him, for He cares for you (1 Peter 5:7).

The Lord will perfect that which concerns you (Psalm 138:8).

12. "All God's Ways are Peace"

The sum of Your Word is truth. Those who love Your law [God's word] have great peace, and nothing causes them to stumble.
PSALM 119:160, 165

This verse doesn't say that those who love God's word will *never* have problems; rather, it says that they will have great peace. Nothing (no matter how difficult) will cause them to stumble. What a wonderful promise this is. In the midst of our circumstances, the Lord meets us right where we are, and sends His word to make His will plain. He always finds a way to make Himself heard. In scripture reading, or His word written on our hearts, or through verses that He refreshes in our minds, or maybe a sermon or a teaching, or a friend, spouse, or complete stranger, God zeroes in on our need and speaks directly to our situation.

All [God's] ways are filled with peace (Proverbs 3:17).

Those who love Thy Law have great peace (Psalm 119:165).

Thou wilt keep Him in perfect peace whose mind is stayed on Thee (Isaiah 26:3, KJV).

Be still, and know that I am God (Psalm 46:10, KJV).

13. "God will make You Know"

Who is the man who fears [reveres] the Lord?
He will instruct him in the way he should choose…
*He will **make them know** His covenant [His word].*
PSALM 25:12, 14

The pressure from all of our striving is off! Scripture does not require 80% effort on our part before God steps in with the remaining 20%. The psalmist tells us the truth of the matter. For those who revere the Lord, God *will make him know* the way he should choose. The Lord has plainly told us that He knows we are dust. He has compassion on us. He understands our total inability to sort through life's difficulties and find His will. That's why the Lord takes responsibility for revealing His chosen path to us.

14. "We ARE Children of Light"

For you were formerly darkness,
but now you are Light in the Lord;
Walk as children of Light.
Ephesians 5:8

A few years after Dave's death, I was chatting over lunch with a senior vice-president, and our conversation turned to a discussion of this verse: *Walk as children of Light.* We both wondered what that might mean and we began to chart out our day in the form of a pie chart on an extra napkin. After a few minutes we had wedges of our pie chart labeled: career, family, sleep, social, recreational, and last of all, Christian life/church. Then the Lord shed His light on us and we were immediately caught in two ways:

First, we had relegated Christ to a slim wedge, effectively excluding Him from the bulk of our lives. The wedge was so thin, in fact, that it seemed inconsequential. But scripture does not use pie charts to describe our lives.

Second, we fell into the trap of thinking that only when we are living and acting perfectly, *then* we are Light. Only when we are in church and looking good, then we are Light. With this human logic as our standard, we concluded that we were not "walking in Light" much at all.

But scripture tells us that we *are* Light with a capital "L" *all the time* and in *every* aspect of our life. In reality, anything and everything in our lives that comes from God *is* Light. Christ *in us* shines forth His Light wherever we walk, in every wedge of our lives. In fact, the wedges we created on that napkin are delusions. Our lives are not constructed of cubicles that can be weighed and balanced, but rather a living whole. Christ *is* Light and that divine Light shines into everything we do.

For example, when I get a thought to read my Bible, pray, or fellowship with other Christians, we would all agree that this is sourced in God and is Light. But how about recognizing when I am wrong and apologizing for my anger to a coworker who does not yet know the Lord? Can God shine His Light into the world in this way? He surely does. That person being apologized to sees a person (just like them) who has a living relationship with God.

In my experience, Christ's Light often shines brightest, not when we are living perfectly, but when He is dealing with some aspect of our flesh. Light doesn't mean that our flesh never shows itself, but rather that we are people who hate the flesh when it does.

15. "Falling Short of Expectations"

There is no fear in love, but perfect love casts out fear.
1 JOHN 4:18

Here is a verse that touched me greatly regarding how I treat employees of the corporation. For years I held the attitude: "Do your job right, or there's the door." Of course, at the same time God was making me mindful that I was nothing more than dust myself *(Psalm 103:14)*, but I held steadfast to my harsh attitude toward others and neglected to have compassion on those around me (even though they were dust just like me). I didn't hesitate to mentally make note of workers who fell short of my expectations. Over time, however, God orchestrated two wondrous miracles in my heart: *First*, He made me increasingly aware of countless personal shortcomings, many of which I would fire myself for, and His mercy for wrapping *me* with His own perfect robe of righteousness as an unmerited gift *(Isaiah 61:10)*! *Second*, He showed me the glaring contrast between my own self-centered, often critical attitude toward employees on the one hand, and His incredible, reassuring, kindness toward me on the other. He was moving me gradually to see every person around me in a whole new light: each one as a unique *trust* given to me from Him.

Increasingly, I desired them to feel the same growing security in their relationship with the company that I was experiencing in my relationship with the Lord. My role as employer consisted of far more than just "getting the company's work done." It also involved nurturing and protecting relationships with others (Christian or not), whom the Lord had gathered together in our workplace family. I became aware of their abilities and weaknesses, and fostered loyalty and quality of work through genuine respect and concern for their well-being.

16. "The True Gospel"

*For of **His fullness** we have all received, and grace
upon grace.*
JOHN 1:16

In recent years, the Lord has brought wonderful nourishing light to this verse. It is the verse that inspired the name *Grace Upon Grace Foundation* for the non-profit foundation that the Lord led me to establish. Our lives are intended by God to be filled to the fullness of Him. This life becomes a joyous opportunity to celebrate each day with Him as Sovereign Lord in our lives. When we get anxious, He provides grace (that is, He provides more of His life in us as an unmerited blessing); and when we worry, or get angry, jealous, or fearful, He provides *grace upon grace*. In other words, He is always providing *more grace* than we need in the situation we find ourselves in. This is His loving way. He fills us with divine love beyond our ability to contain it. This is the true gospel that He draws others to see in us. This is what others desire deep in their hearts: to know this God of *grace upon grace*.

17. "Who Sits behind Our Desk?"

*The seed whose fruit is righteousness is sown **in peace**
by those who make peace.*
JAMES 3:18

So, how do we "make" peace, as James puts it? Simple: by staying on our knees in our hearts before God. People ask me from time to time, "What does it mean to be a

Christian businessperson? How, exactly, do we create a peaceful Christian workplace?" I don't hide the answer from them, but it usually isn't what they expect to hear. The answer is: *we* don't create anything. *It is God who creates it*—and He does so by drawing us to remain on our knees in our hearts before Him. He is overcoming our flesh, our propensity for argument, strife, pride, self-centeredness, and our relentless efforts to "take charge" over our own lives. He is transforming the circumstances and problems in our lives into positive opportunities for growing more of *Christ in us*. He is securing and strengthening our hearts through a deeper knowledge of Himself. In a nutshell: God—in all His greatness, lovingkindness, and practicality—is the One walking in our shoes, sitting behind our desk, and causing those around us, whether conscious of it or not, to perceive His presence and peace in their midst.

18. "Tuning into God's Signals"

In all your ways acknowledge Him, and He will make your paths straight.
PROVERBS 3:6

Do you ever find yourself between that proverbial *rock and hard place*? Not sure which path to take? It's easy to get uptight in such a situation, to think everything is up to us—that we've got to make a move, even when it's not yet clear what that move should be. When our hearts are tuned to the Lord, however—when we are looking for His signals—those endless forks in the road become opportunities to experience more of His life.

I remember one evening as I was preparing to leave work; I noticed a light coming from the office of one of my sons. Aware that he was facing a great difficulty in his personal life, I stood in the hallway, wondering whether or not it would be fitting to drop in and encourage him a bit. Quietly, I looked to the Lord in my spirit, desiring to know what He would have me do. To my surprise, my feet began to turn in the direction of the parking lot, as if set in motion by some unseen force. The answer, though unexpected, was plain: *tonight is not the night.* Once again, the Lord was directing my steps—this time, quite literally!

19. "Making Requests to God"

Be anxious for nothing, but in everything by prayer and supplication with thanksgiving let your requests be made known to God.
PHILIPPIANS 4:6

This verse is not telling us to *try our best* to be free of anxiety; rather, it is stating the condition that results when we take those things that concern us to God in prayer and thanksgiving, knowing He will care for us in everything. It is truly amazing how this works. I can get caught up in obsessing over the pros and cons of a given situation or decision. But the moment I turn from those human calculations and take the situation or concern to God in prayer and supplication (like a humble request) with thanksgiving, I feel the anxiety lift off me. God is guarding my heart and mind against that anxiety. Peace is reestablished within me once more. This may seem strange if you haven't tried it, but the more you practice this, the more you will grow in life-experiences of how this actually works.

And the peace of God, which surpasses all comprehension, will guard your hearts and your minds in Christ Jesus (Philippians 4:7).

Wisdom will enter your heart and knowledge will be pleasant to your soul (Proverbs 2:10).

20. "Seeing is in the Tasting"

O taste and see that the Lord is good.
PSALM 34:8A

If the psalmist wanted us to "see that the Lord is good," why didn't he just say that directly? Why did he go the extra step of adding the element of tasting? Under the inspiration of the Holy Spirit, the psalmist was describing a *deeper level of experience* than what you can achieve only by sight. An observer can look upon an object, but that object is inherently detached and separated from the observer. The psalmist didn't want us to look upon God as an object, but to experience God as nourishment, to taste and internalize Him. Then, over time, you get a "taste" for God; and you find yourself craving more and more of His presence.

Besides you [God], *I desire nothing on earth* (Psalm 73:25).

21. "God's Radar System"

For the word of God is living and active and sharper than any two-edged sword, and piercing as far as the division

of soul and spirit, of both joints and marrow, and able to judge the thoughts and intentions of the heart.
HEBREWS 4:12

Scripture is God's divine "reticular activator." What's that? According to scientific understanding, the Reticular Activator is part of the brain that functions like a radar system that is on the lookout 24 hours a day, 7 days a week, for things that are: (i) familiar, (ii) unusual, or (iii) problematic. When our brain detects any of these things on a subconscious level, it sends a message to the conscious side of the brain that says, "Hey, wake up! There's something you need to pay attention to." We've all experienced this phenomenon in our lives. Let's say you are thinking about buying a new car and you've gone to look at various models. By the end of the day, you've focused your attention on one model and color that you really like. Then to your surprise, over the coming week, you begin to see that model car all over town. It seems like everyone owns it. That is your reticular activator radar system kicking in.

God uses scripture in the same way. For example, once God brought Psalm 15 to my attention in connection with lying to my wife (*see* chapter six), it didn't stop there. Almost on a daily basis, I "discovered" other business practices, which I had followed for years and considered the "wise" and "business savvy" approach to some process or another, now began to appear suspect. I'll give you an example of this in the next reading.

22. "Seeing God's Love in Practice"

Hear the cries of the field workers whom you have cheated
of their pay. Their cries have reached the ears of the Lord
of Hosts.
JAMES 5:4 TLB

In the early years of our company, we picked up the
notion from some business magazine or other that the best
way to improve a company's cash flow on a short-term or
temporary basis was to delay payment to vendors. This was
easy to do, fully in your control to implement (that is, there
was no need for a bank application and approval process).
In my mind, I agreed with the article. It just made "good
business sense" for those vendors to wait an extra thirty
or forty-five days after the invoice's due date; surely such
a short delay wouldn't hurt them, and it seemed to me like
an excellent way to generate extra capital easily. After all, I
would use the funds to expand the business which, in turn,
would then increase business to those same vendors. From
that demented perspective, it was a "win-win" proposition
for the vendor as well, even though they were not partici-
pating in this growth strategy voluntarily.

God, however, was actively making it clear that much of
what I considered "good business practices" were actually
at serious odds with His truth. Bible verses that I had never
dreamed related to those practices were suddenly coming
alive with new relevance. Take for example, this verse in
James. Why I was reading James at that time I don't recall.
Whatever the human reason, it was God's drawing me to
the verse. As I read James 5:4, you can imagine what God

was speaking to me. Here is what the particular message from this verse sounded like in *Daryl's heart version*:

> *[Listen Daryl], hear the cries of the fieldworkers [and all your vendors] whom you have cheated [by delaying payment] of their pay; their cries have reached the ears of the Lord of Hosts.*

It seemed that, in the Lord's economy, there was an intimate connection between being honest and paying bills on time. God's truth wasn't merely concerned with *whether* we paid our bills, but *when* we paid them! As this truth took hold in my heart, I began to spend more time attending to how our company honored its financial commitments and less time worrying about how many times a day I shared my Christian testimony. In fact, as paying on time became a top priority, the Lord clarified my thinking to recognize that the only task He had given me was not complicated; it was to act in a respectful, consistent, honest, forthright, and punctual manner with vendors and suppliers. This is how God desired to show these people His love through me. Obviously, this divine testimony far exceeded my hypocritical testimony of cheating them of their money with one hand, while patting them on the back with the other, and inviting them to my church.

23. "The Benefits of Tribulation"

> *We also glory in tribulations, knowing that tribulation produces perseverance; and perseverance, character; and character, hope. Now hope does not disappoint, because*

the love of God has been poured out in our hearts by the
Holy Spirit who was given to us.
ROMANS 5:3–5 NKJV

Each of us acquires a cumulative personal history of God's goodness in our lives. We look back to the myriad of times He has uniquely demonstrated His faithfulness to us; and experiencing His truth in our circumstances establishes His word more firmly within us. We are thus attracted to delve more deeply into His word and this increases the measure of our peace even more. One could say that our daily problems and decisions facilitate that peace, because they cause us to focus on who God is and how He has promised to direct us in very specific ways.

Consider it all joy, my brethren, when you encounter various trials, knowing that the testing of your faith produces endurance. And let endurance have its perfect result, so that you may be perfect and complete, lacking in nothing (James 1:2–4).

24. "All-Inclusive Salvation"

Are you so foolish? Having begun by the Spirit, are you now being perfected by the flesh?
GALATIANS 3:3

Paul has a way with words, doesn't he? But he's right. Where do we get this idea that the Christian life is a product of what we do? Or, as Paul put it, that having begun in the Spirit, we are now being perfected by the flesh. Isn't the God who lives *within us* the same awesome and All-knowing Creator of the whole Universe—the *entire* life, light, wisdom, and power of the Almighty Trinity? And didn't He, of His own accord, choose to reveal Himself to us long before we were even born—not on the basis of any merit of ours, but when we (yes, you and I!) were still held captive by *the power of darkness* (Colossians 1:13)—still *separate from Christ* (Ephesians 2:12), *dead in [our] trespasses,* and *by nature children of wrath* (Ephesians 2:1, 3)?

*By grace you have been saved through faith; and that **not of yourselves**, it is the gift of God; not as a result of works, so that no one may boast* (Ephesians 2:8-9).

*God, being rich in mercy, because of His great love with which He loved us, **even when we were dead**...made us alive together with Christ* (Ephesians 2:4-5).

*For He **rescued** us from the domain of darkness, and transferred us to the kingdom of His beloved Son* (Colossians 1:13).

Think about it: if we did truly comprehend the enormous lengths to which the Lord went to redeem us from our pitiful, lost condition—the merciful and wholly *unilateral* initiative He willingly undertook on our behalf—would it ever occur to us to try to "add" something to that? Isn't it far more likely that the sheer, amazing joy of such knowledge would put an end to all our struggling and striving? And deal a death blow once and for all to the likes of guilt, fear, and stress of every kind? In 1 Corinthians 1:30, we read, "But by His doing you are in Christ Jesus, who *became to us* wisdom from God, and righteousness and sanctification, and redemption." Sanctification refers to our "Christian growth." Scripture tells us that this growth is not something we do, but who we have living within us.

25. "Christ in the Details"

*For if **while we were enemies** we were reconciled to God through the death of His Son, **much more, having been reconciled**, we shall be **saved by His life**.*
Romans 5:10

If God is great enough and loving enough to call us out of total darkness and depravity into the light of believing in His Son Jesus as our only hope and salvation, then doesn't it stand to reason that He is also great and loving enough to take control of all our circumstances? Isn't He great and loving enough to provide His children with a path of peace in directing our lives? Yes, He is that great and that loving. It takes every bit of stress out of our lives.

26. "What's the Truth?"

He who walks with integrity, and works righteousness, and speaks truth in his heart.
Psalm 15:2

I shared with you how God used scripture to expose how I was lying to my wife and failing to care for her. It wasn't long after that lesson that He began to challenge deeply established habits in other areas of my life, particularly in business. How many of the words I spoke during the day to others were actually intended only to pacify, or avoid blame or personal inconvenience in the workplace? And by extension, how honest—truly honest—was our company when it came to communicating with its customers?

Like any business, no matter how hard we try to avoid it, we receive a certain number of complaints as part of our ongoing service business. No matter how diligent a company is to operate in a manner where complaints never happen—they still occasionally occur. But for most of my career, I just assumed that those problems were seldom, if ever, our fault. In fact, it was imperative that they *not* be perceived by anyone as "our fault." So, when they *were* our fault, I held to the firm conviction that we should *never* admit to the error, on the basis that it would surely lower customer confidence in the company.

As a result, I grew robotic in delivering the same defensive replies year after year, hoping to avoid blame, ostensibly for the purpose of protecting the bottom line. I not only conducted myself in this manner, but also met with various senior corporate staff members to brainstorm (often for hours) on what "spin" we should put on "our story" in order to save face. Of course, we didn't use these derogatory terms to describe what we were doing, but that is what it was—nothing but *spin* and *storytelling*.

As the words from Psalm 15, "walk with integrity," continued to come alive and resonate within me, that old impulse to cover up our errors, with the legerdemain of spin, seemed increasingly trite. Instead of a compulsion to shift blame for problems to others, which assumed that others were *always* at fault, I began to experience a growing freedom, even desire, to face head-on the truth of what others had to say.

This came to a climactic turning point in a business meeting one day, with no small amount of personal discomfort I might add. I was listening to two of my colleagues discuss how best to cover up a recent mistake we had made at the corporate office. Then, one of them turned to me and asked, "Daryl, do you think our franchisees will buy this story?" I felt pierced in my heart by the question. God had brought me to see something more important than whether our franchisees would "buy our story." For the first time, the only answer I wanted to give was the one flowing out of the growing peace of Christ in my heart: "You know," I said, "I'd really prefer that you just tell the franchisees what actually happened."

And that's been our policy ever since.

Today, when employees ask how they should respond to customer complaints, I have only one reply: "What's the truth? Just say that." And if they continue to press me with further details about the situation, I usually ask them to clarify what they are asking me: "Are you asking how to fix the actual problem, or whether to admit that we made a mistake in the first place? If it's the latter, then please listen to me—*simply tell them the truth*."

Here is something else I learned from all of this—something that surprised me because it was so counter-intuitive to my old thinking. Many of the difficulties which used to eat up so much of my time and energy no longer required my involvement. Many of these problems were the very matters that kept me working late and missing being home on time. But now, if our policy was simply to tell the truth, there was no longer the need for multiple-hour strategy sessions to come up with the right spin on a palatable story. *Truth* is what it is. In terms of business policy, it is an amazingly efficient filter and a real time saver!

And here is the biggest surprise of all for me. I just shared with you my greatest fear—that if we admitted to making a mistake it would lower customer confidence and damage the company's reputation. I could fill this book with stories of how the exact opposite is true. In reality, who were we kidding through all our spinning? Nobody! Once we began to *walk with integrity and speak the truth* regardless of the consequences, the company's reputation grew more firm.

The secret of the Lord is for those who fear [revere] Him, and He will make them know His covenant (Psalm 25:14).

27. "God's Perspective"

For He Himself knows our frame; He is mindful that we are but dust.
PSALM 103:14

You and I are no more than dust. God knows this. As we are drawn by God to set our hearts upon Him, He will never stop reaching out to us. One way or another, you can trust that God always—clearly—makes us to know His will for us day by day. He is the Potter and we are the clay. He has promised to craft us into a vessel that brings glory to Him. In this we have no boast *(1 Corinthians 1:31).*

28. "Wisdom in the Counsel of Many"

Where there is no guidance the people fall, but in abundance of counselors there is victory.
PROVERBS 11:14

I used to believe for years that it was my individual responsibility to have *all the answers* in directing the company through *every* situation. I had to make decisions on a regular basis: how to resolve a persistent problem involving a major client; whether to promote a particular employee or hire a new operations manager; or where to cut expenses. As long as I felt solely responsible for these decisions, my life was dominated with worry, turmoil, anxiety, and stress. Every conflict at work appeared to be an obstacle to my leadership and a threat to my respect as a leader. Yet, I held tenaciously to the belief that the mark of a successful business leader was his or her ability to make swift and decisive decisions. I deeply feared to leave any matter unresolved for more than a few hours or a day. Ironically, it was my dread of *not* making the "right decision" which frequently drove me to make the hasty or imprudent ones.

That's where *wisdom in the counsel of many* comes to the rescue. The Lord has brought me today to highly value the input and opinions of others. Contrary to demonstrating weakness, it is the mark of a wise leader to consider all viable options prior to making a decision. Almost on a daily basis, I seek the counsel of one or more of my vice-presidents and senior staff. These folks spend their day working in the nitty-gritty trenches of the business and have valuable experience to share.

29. "From the Mouth...Grace Speaks"

Let no unwholesome word proceed from your mouth, but only such a word as is good for edification according to the need of the moment, so that it will give grace to those who hear.
EPHESIANS 4:29

When it comes to peace in the workplace, this verse has been a huge influence on my life. Whether I am dealing with a disgruntled employee or an employee whose performance is below expectations, or perhaps something that is disappointing in one of my kids. This verse is a big-time reality check on my words. Will the words I speak come across as *encouraging* to the listener related to the matter at hand; or *discouraging* and judgmental, focused on their perceived failure? The Lord has impressed upon me the value of *pondering* my words before speaking to a difficult, stressful, or disappointing situation. How am I going to address this in a way that has the chance of encouraging the listener versus discouraging him or her? Proverbs 15:28 declares, "The heart of the righteous *ponders* how to answer, but the mouth of the wicked pours out evil things."

It not only governs *my* speech, but has a significant "passing-on" effect in the entire workplace. As I communicate with senior staff in this manner, those same individuals increasingly deal with those accountable to them in a similar fashion. I lived half of my life voicing my displeasure to others, believing that a bit of bullying was the best way to achieve my goals. All that accomplished was a workplace full of anxiety and stress. It really had no value and didn't change a thing. For the last thirty years, the Lord has been teaching me that providing a workplace that *encourages* the employee toward what you desire for them to do is vastly more effective.

30. "Healing Grievances"

Let all bitterness and wrath and anger and clamor and
slander be put away from you, along with all malice.
EPHESIANS 4:31

I end this book with this verse because it was a major word from God in turning the office workplace from stress to peace. Of course, we can never in our own effort put away bitterness and malice, that's why this aspect is such a wonderful way to grow in Christ. The first thing the Lord touched my heart regarding this verse was my penchant for keeping negative things pent-up within me; or, to say it another way, in my willingness to harbor grievances toward an employee in a way that allowed those grievances to pile up in my heart and mind. Then when those grievances reached a certain level, I'd come into work and tell the person: "You're fired!" Of course, they were shocked because my blunt termination announcement would be the first time they heard that there was a problem.

Now days, I don't want any more surprises for employees. If I'm disappointed in something about a particular employee's work as it pertains to his or her job or job future, I will discuss it with that employee within 24 to 48 hours. That way, it doesn't have a chance to fester in me and together we can begin to work on a solution that improves the employee's job performance. I'm driven to talk to them about it for two reasons: *First,* out of fairness to the employee. No one deserves to be surprised with a termination of their employment because God has never treated me that way. *Second,* because I don't want to let it fester in me, like some caustic brew, and affect *my* peace in Christ. Now I work with people throughout the office *without* any deep-seated anger or resentment toward anyone. It makes a big difference in the level of peace others feel as well.

If you enjoyed the fellowship contained in this book, *A Simplified Life,* and want to know more about God's grace for you, then you are invited to *listen* to videos or audios of Daryl's Bible studies, or *join in* on discussions in a community of fellowship focused on Christ (and His loving mercy and grace for us).

Go to:
Grace Upon Grace Foundation website:
www.gugf.org

CPSIA information can be obtained at www.ICGtesting.com
Printed in the USA
BVOW08s1115101213

338663BV00002B/4/P